FROM THE REMNANTS
A Story of Light and Hope

Cathy Schrader
As told to Rosemarie Fitzsimmons

Copyright © 2016 The Portrait Writer, LLC

Published by: Portrait Writer Publishing
All rights reserved. No part of this publication may be reproduced, stored in a retrieval system, or transmitted in any form or by any means, electronic, mechanical, photocopying, recording, or otherwise, without the prior permission of the copyright holder.

ISBN-13:978-1533510884
ISBN-10:1533510881

Cover design by Brad Harding

Special thanks to Mary Scro, Michele Halbeisen and other readers/editors for their editing assistance and insightful advice.

Author: Cathy Schrader
Cathyschrader16@gmail.com
(304) 314-4293
www.fromtheremnants.com
Social Media: From the Remnants

Writer: Rosemarie Fitzsimmons
The Portrait Writer, LLC
http://www.rosethestoryteller.com
rosefitz.portraitwriter@gmail.com

DEDICATION

This book is dedicated to my little angels,
Tiffany Ann (Aug 7, 1991)
and
Matthew Paul (April 22, 1992),
whose short lives birthed a ministry
that has impacted people across the nation
and in parts of the world.

In Honor of my Mother, Phyllis Berkenkemper
(June 18, 1936 – July 28, 2016)
Whose love, support and guidance are felt
throughout the pages of this book.

Author's Note:

The following is a true story, told to the best of my recollection, and validated both through research where feasible and through consulting with others involved. Conversations recounted in this story are fictional, as they would be impossible to duplicate all these years later, however, they represent the essence of discussions that did occur. The events recounted here did occur; however, the names and details of some events and individuals have been changed to protect the identities of those involved.

Cathy Schrader

DEFINING MOMENT

*"For I know the plans I have for you,"
declares the Lord, "plans to prosper you and not to harm you,
plans to give you hope and a future. -- Jeremiah 29:11*

    I believe we all experience defining moments in our lives, moments where we've been stripped down to our barest selves, when time seems to stop and darkness threatens to overwhelm us. Moments where our hearts must fight to force just one more breath into us, or to make us take that next step. Moments that could crush us if we let them.
    We have no control over the moments themselves. They are powerful, unavoidable, and often life-shattering. They may have built up over months or years, such as that moment a divorce becomes inevitable, or they can sneak into our lives like a thief in the night with an unexpected word from a doctor and wrench something precious from our arms. I experienced both at once, and more.
    Sometimes, perhaps again and again, or even years after we've been shattered, the slightest reminder can rush us back to that

moment, which we re-live in vivid detail, and we become crushed anew with the realization that we may have moved on, but we haven't healed.

What is it that makes or breaks a person during these times of darkness? Why do some people fall into an abyss of alcohol, or sex, or fall prey to the myriad other vices that entrap and enslave us when we search for solace in their midst? How is it that others stand and push forward against the gale-force winds of doubt and pain and somehow triumph?

I believe it's our faith. In that defining moment, we must either believe there is One who can help us through our storm and we turn toward him, or we lose hope and turn away, resigned to fighting the battle on our own. And if we chose to fight on our own, we will never truly heal.

That said, it's not easy to believe God cares, particularly while we're suffocating under the weight of sadness and fear. The journey from dark to light is rarely without struggle. God beckons to us from his mountain top, and one doesn't usually climb a mountain without acquiring a few scrapes and bruises, perhaps even stepping off a cliff once or twice. However, the journey is absolutely worth the effort and God's coaching is relentless and loving. Surprisingly, I've found that I tend to be most attentive to God's instructions during those moments when I'm clinging to a ledge by my fingertips waiting for help to arrive. Perhaps because that's sometimes what it takes for me to finally admit I DO need his help.

This is the story of my defining moment and the journey that ensued. It's a story that could have ended in the depths of despair, if not for a God who loves us way too much to let us have our own way.

It is a story about light and hope.

MEANT TO BE

    God planned a purpose for me from the start, which is evident in the lengthy but futile battle Satan fought to prevent my existence.
    As Mom tells it, Satan started meddling in my life long before she even knew about me. Her first pregnancy ended in a miscarriage with such heavy hemorrhaging that the alarmed doctors told her she could never carry a child, and that to try would put her own life at risk. Naturally, this frightened my dad, who quickly obtained the three-doctor approval form required at the time to authorize a tubal ligation and prevent future pregnancies. Fortunately for me and my siblings, Mom refused to sign it.
    "It's not up to you or the doctors," she told him." It's up to God." I'm betting she had her arms crossed and stubborn defiance written all over her face when she told him. That's just how she gets when someone tries to make decisions for her.
    My oldest sister, Terry, entered the world prematurely, weighing only two pounds. She had Dad's exotic olive complexion, jet black hair, and Mom's sweet face. She spent her first several months in ICU, healthy, but weak. When Mom and Dad finally brought her to their small home in the Baltimore suburbs, the big world overpowered her

tiny lungs. She developed pneumonia, and then the German Measles. During the ordeal, her fragile little brain reached temperatures above 106 degrees. Mentally, she would not mature past 4 months old, and she has required constant care throughout her life.

Mom kept fighting. Despite a second dangerous miscarriage, she wanted to give my father a son because all his brothers had sons. She prayed for a little boy who would look just like my dad, and became pregnant with my brother Mitchell. The doctors warned she would not carry him to term.

She would not be swayed, but made her position clear. "I prayed for a son and God will give me a son." That took care of *that*.

Had Mitch been born on his due date, he would have shared his birthday with Dad and my grandfather. However, he had other plans and barely made it to seven months before bursting into the world. Despite the rush, he arrived healthy, and he did, indeed, look just like Dad.

My parents kept Terry at home and worked crazy hours to ensure someone would always be home to care for her. When Mitch should have started walking and talking, he did nothing. The doctors determined he'd been copying Terry, which could severely affect his development. It broke Mom and Dad's heart to place Terry in a facility, but they wanted the best for both their children and decided this would allow Terry the 24-hour care and attention she needed and create a healthier environment for Mitch's development. Within a month, Mitch was running through the house playing and starting to talk. My mother, now emboldened by this proof that she could have healthy children, pressed her luck. My sister Tammi entered the world at five pounds, the largest of the Berkenkemper children and the only one of us who didn't have to spend time in ICU.

When I came along, the doctors encouraged Mom to abort. "She won't make it," they said. "You have to think of the children you have at home."

Mom once again refused, and she told them that I deserved the same chance at life as she did and it was up to God whether I lived—not the doctors.

During her pregnancy, Mom developed severe morning sickness and accepted a prescription from her doctor for a new medication on the market, but her body rejected it. She couldn't keep even the tiniest amount in her system. This proved to be a merciful blessing, as researchers later determined that this particular medication caused serious birth defects in unborn children. Satan's attempts to harm me were thwarted again.

Mom persevered, and carried me seven months. I made my debut in a Baltimore hospital room in February 1968 on my Grandma's birthday. Despite Satan's persistent meddling, the doctors prevailed that day. Not only a preemie, but a breech baby as well, I had to be gently repositioned with forceps time and time again before the doctors could deliver me.

I spent weeks in ICU before the doctors deemed my lungs strong enough to sustain me, and they sent me home. They hadn't counted on the Meddler, who ensured I returned almost immediately with pneumonia. Although Mom sat by me as long as she could, she had to leave me that evening to tend to her family back home. Before she could return, however, repercussions from an event that began more than 900 miles away reached Baltimore and nearly destroyed it. Mom would have to wait almost three weeks before she could hold me again.

You see, that day someone named James Earl Ray shot and killed Martin Luther King, Jr. outside his hotel room in Memphis, Tenn. Shock waves rippled across the nation, spurring riots in many of America's larger cities. Only the rioters ventured outside their homes. In Baltimore, authorities closed the schools and turned them into make-shift jails. Mom could only stare helplessly at the television as the city burned.

More than 1,100 Army and National Guard soldiers streamed in to take up armed posts throughout the city. Mom prayed the hospital would be spared in the violence, although one news story told of a priest being beaten up at the hospital door, and another showed cars and ambulances in the area being overturned.

Every day during the riots, Mom called the hospital to check on me, always receiving the same message: "Your baby's fine, ma'am. We're all okay."

Finally, after enduring weeks of looting, burning, mob rule, and more than 5,300 arrests, Baltimore settled down. As soon as officials lifted the travel ban, Mom and Dad rushed back into the city with everyone else. Downtown looked like a war zone, with many of its busi-

From the Remnants

nesses reduced to smoking heaps, and with tons of debris making the roads nearly impassable. But they wouldn't be deterred. They picked their way through the glass- and rubble-filled streets to get to me.

I came home and we lived near my dad's family until I turned two, and then we moved to the West Virginia farmhouse where my mother had been raised. With the exception of my fourth- and twelfth-grade years, I grew up in that farmhouse.

I met Chris in the third grade, in Mrs. Trimble's gifted class. I barely gave him any notice at first, not knowing he would become my best friend and confidant for the rest of my life. Looking back, I know now that God put him there because I'd need him for stability, later, when my world crumbled.

We had to earn our way into Mrs. Trimble's classroom, first, by establishing ourselves as high achievers, and then, by finishing our regular class work quickly each day. We couldn't turn in mediocre class work, or we'd no longer qualify for the program. Essentially, making good grades gave us the keys to the kingdom. Chris and I had no problem with that—we couldn't get bad grades if we tried, we were both that driven.

One funny aspect to that . . . I nearly didn't get into the gifted class. I'd taken many tests to determine my eligibility, but the instructors told my mom I kept failing. This had everyone baffled because they knew by my class scores I was more than capable. Mom and I went to this meeting with the testing folks, and she let me explain in front of them.

"Cathy, why do you suppose you're doing so poorly on the gifted tests when you take them?"

I hesitated. I hadn't counted on them seeing through my plan.

"Well, um . . . you see, it's on account of Russell."

"The boy in Special Ed?" Mom looked confused.

"Yes. His class dances and sings a lot. They have a lot of fun."

"Okay..." Even the instructors seemed puzzled. I could practically feel their eyes on me.

"Well, I asked him what he had to do to get into that class, and he said he failed a lot of tests. I figured if I failed too, I'd be able to play with Russell."

Cathy Schrader

I'm pretty sure Mom had to fight to hide the smile, but the head instructor laughed out loud.

"That's one smart little girl," he said. "She had us all stumped."

I retook the tests and passed with flying colors. My world would never be the same.

Mrs. Trimble, the greatest teacher ever, had a knack for bringing the best out in every student. Her classroom comprised the school's brightest minds from grades three through eight, and her assignments challenged us to excel beyond even what we knew we could accomplish.

I gave a half-hearted effort to my first gifted-class assignment, accustomed to such efforts being considered superb in the regular classroom. She looked it over then handed it right back.

"Now, do this to your potential."

She said it with a smile, but I felt crushed nonetheless, primarily because I knew I'd let her down. I never forgot that moment. It inspired me to always do my best work, an attitude that propelled me through some difficult tasks throughout my life.

In Mrs. Trimble's classroom, all assignments became big productions and capitalized on our greatest strengths. For our core group, Chris and I provided the artistic talent, my sister Tammi excelled in photography, and our friend Steve added his passion for technology. Together we could turn just about anything into a large-scale adventure.

One day we latched onto the idea of making puppets. Naturally, with puppets one needed a theater, scripts, background scenes, and a marketing strategy, because, of course, we would be performing. Mrs. Trimble encouraged us by acquiring an enormous refrigerator box that made the perfect theater.

During our theater show preparation, Steve, Chris, and I kindled our friendship. Chris was so funny, we hit it off immediately. We laughed and joked as we wrote the scripts, cracking ourselves up more than anyone else. . .

"And then the goat said that's a *baaaad* idea." Chris wrote with one hand and worked the small goat puppet with the other.

"Well then, Mr. Groundhog is going to China!" I made my puppet dig against the table top, then slipped him underneath. "Hey, it's dark down here!"

From the Remnants

We giggled and wrote until the play was ready, then the three of us piled our tiny bodies into the brightly painted "theater." We fit perfectly, with room to spare for switching out the poster-board backdrop scenes we'd hung on hooks in front of us so only the puppets could be seen. We acted out The Groundhog's Story to a beaming Mrs. Trimble. It may not have been Broadway material, but we enjoyed ourselves immensely.

"Wonderful." She clapped when we finished. "Now you must take this performance on tour!"

And so we did. Somewhere between drawing up playbill posters and lugging the giant cardboard roadshow from class to class over the next few weeks, the three of us, but especially Chris and I, became pals. When school let out for the summer, we spent a lot of time together, both at each other's homes and in the newspaper office that Chris' dad owned. I liked having a friend who understood me, and who shared my fondness for art and scary movies. However, as summer waned, Mom and Dad hit me with their plans to move back to Maryland.

Chris and I said our good-byes in a matter-of-fact manner. We'd only known each other a short time. I knew I'd miss him, but figured I'd make other friends in my new school.

We moved to Essex, a small town just north of Baltimore. I don't remember much from that year, but one person I'll always remember is my friend, Sophia, through whom I learned that life is not always as carefree or as fair as it should be, and sometimes innocent people get hurt.

The first time I realized Sophia led a less-than-ideal life, we were standing in line outside our classroom, waiting for the morning bell to ring and the teacher to swing open the door. Neither Sophia, already an unusually quiet girl, nor her younger sister, Grace, had spoken during our walk to school, and they declined to join the other children laughing and running on the playground. Now she stood quietly, looking almost fearful. I tried to talk to her, but she just stared at the door, as if willing it to open.

Just before the bell rang, her mother came storming around the corner wearing what looked like slept-in evening clothes. Her bedraggled hair fluttered wildly behind her, and streaks of makeup, clearly from the previous day, had smeared across her cheekbones. I felt Sophia tense up beside me and for a brief moment wondered if I could hide her, but it was too late. As the enraged woman yanked Sophia out of line, I looked into my friend's tear-filled eyes and saw a resigned spirit. Some of us followed them back to their car, watching helplessly from the edge of the school yard as Sophia's mother landed blow after blow on the poor girl's body.

By age 10, Sophia had already tried to commit suicide three times.

We played together after school because Sophia's mother worked during the day. I never met her father. Sophia and Grace lived in fear of making mistakes, and made sure to get home on time every evening. One rainy, miserable evening, she came to our house sobbing. She'd gone home to find a locked house and mom and Grace gone.

"You can stay here," Mom said. "We'll try to call her."

Sophia worked herself into such an anxious state, Mom drove her back to check the house three or four times that night. Finally, after Mom wrote a note explaining that she was safe, Sophia agreed to stay. We did our homework together and tried to have fun, but the cloud hanging over her would not subside. In the morning, I loaned Sophia some of my clothes and we were nearly ready for school when we heard the heavy stomping on the front walk and a loud, angry pounding on the front door. Sophia raced half way up the hall stairs as my mother went to answer the door, then Sophia turned.

"Don't let her have me." She pleaded, her white-knuckled fingers clinging to the wooden stair rail. "Please don't let her have me."

I could almost see Mom's wheels turning as she weighed her options. I'd told her about witnessing Sophia's beating. Perhaps she thought she could diffuse the situation. She steeled herself with a deep breath, then opened the door, smiling. "Hi Bev, I hope you don't mind—"

"Shut up! Where's my daughter?" Sophia's mom burst in and stood at the foot of the stairs. "Get down here right now Missy, if you know what's good for you."

I wanted to grab Sophia as she edged down the stairs, still clinging to the rails. I wanted to put myself between them, as if I could have stopped anything. Instead, I stood next to Mom, both of us watching in powerless silence as they walked away. Sophia did not come to school that day, or the next.

Another time, Sophia came to the house with poor little Grace sobbing at her side. Grace had lost her doll-baby, and Sophia didn't have to tell me what that meant. I saw it written on her face. I went out with them, and together we traced Grace's steps. We stared into every trash can, combed every inch of ground, and checked the crook of every tree between our houses and the nearby park, and to the school and back. Nothing. As dusk settled in, we returned to their house. Sophia nudged her sister up the stairs and then looked at me.

"You can't come in." She followed her sister into the house.

A day or so later, when I asked if they were all right, Sophia showed me Grace's back. The poor girl had been beaten so hard I could make out lines in her skin from the shirt she'd been wearing. Sophia said clothing fibers had become ingrained in Grace's back, and she'd had to soak them out. I told Mom about that as well.

Sophia called our house at nearly midnight a few nights after that incident. Yet another storm raged outside and she and her sister had been left alone inside. I sat on the stairs listening to Mom talk calmly to her on the phone, knowing that we couldn't do the logical thing, which would be to pick them up and bring them here.

"Get the dog and the three of you go upstairs and wait in a back room." Despite her soothing voice, Mom looked angrier than I'd ever seen her. "The storm will pass soon; I promise you'll be okay."

Child Protective Services stepped in the next day. I don't know if Mom called or another neighbor, but the girls were taken into foster care. I thought all would get better then, but when the phone again rang in the middle of the night. I barely recognized Sophia's voice.

"My mom found us. We're going to Texas." Her hushed, choking tears nearly broke my heart. "I just wanted to say good-bye."

Crushed to the depths of my 10-year-old soul, I hung up the phone swearing that one day I'd find her.

Even if I have to hire a detective.

I cried for days and worried for years. Something in me needed to know she was okay. My family left Maryland that summer, which was a bittersweet move for me. As much as I enjoyed West Virginia, I hated leaving without knowing whether I'd ever see Sophia again. Mom said all we can do is pray about it and believe God will take care of her, and so I did. It would be many years before I learned whether he heard me.

Mom's faith has always been strong, particularly since the candle incident. She not only believes God sees everything and cares deeply about us, but she knows from experience that when he tells us to do something, we'd better do it. I was quite small when the candle incident occurred, but Tammi and Mitch were old enough to remember. It became one of our favorite stories, and she told it often, particularly when we'd find ourselves in a tight spot and think perhaps God wasn't on our side. The candle story reminded that although sometimes our lives seem to make little sense, God always knows what he's doing. Mom's story became such a vital part of my upbringing that I'm going to include it here.

I could narrate the tale, but it seems to lose something in the third person, so I'll let Mom tell you how it happened…

THE CANDLE

By Phyllis Berkenkemper

We were living in West Virginia, and the children were very young. I worked for a state Early Childhood Development Center, connecting needy families with available resources. Every day I'd watch through the window out to the waiting area, where I saw people of all walks of life. I wanted to help them all, but not all can be helped.

Helen, a young mother of two boys, came to the center often. She spent many hours waiting in the reception area while her boys participated in a program we offered. Although we could meet basic needs for her family, the deep sadness in Helen's eyes told me her needs went way beyond anything physical we could give her.

One day a box arrived containing two decorative candles I'd ordered from a catalog, thinking they would brighten up our front desk area for the Christmas season. Inside the box I found one candle I'd ordered, and one I hadn't. The second candle was far more beautiful than anything I remembered seeing in the catalog. White, with specks of silver and sequin-like red dots scattered through it. I found the candle mesmerizing.

From the Remnants

Others were drawn to it as well. I set it on the reception counter for all to see. Many people who passed through that office asked where I bought it. I told them the name of the company, but the mystery deepened. That company didn't make that candle. When I called to address the mix-up, thinking this candle surely cost more than I'd paid, they apologized profusely and said they couldn't identify the candle I described. I even sent them a picture, because I wanted to order more, but they replied, "There's no candle like that in our inventory."

People offered to buy the candle from me. My daughter Tammi saw it when she came to visit me at work and asked if she could have it. My answer was the same to everyone.

"I'm sorry, this one is special, and I cannot find another like it anywhere. I'd like to keep it for myself, it is my favorite."

As Christmas neared, my office became quite busy. For one of our outreach programs, we wrapped gifts that had been donated for some of the needier families in our area, to include Helen's.

I sat by Helen one day and explained what we were doing.

"We have blankets for all three of you, but we'd also like to include a toy or two for the boys." I opened my note pad to write. "What do you think they'd like? Cars and trucks, or are they into sports and perhaps a ball or something?"

"Ma'am, I think they'd enjoy anything." Helen stared down at her fingernails, chewed red down to the quick. "And . . . I thank you so much for the blankets, as we do need them, but . . ." She turned those sad brown eyes toward me and my heart melted. "Ma'am, do you think it would be all right if I asked for something for myself? Nothing big, but just something personal. It's been so long . . . does that make me a bad person?"

I put my hand on her shoulder and tried to reassure her with some gentle pats. "Of course it doesn't, Helen. Don't you worry, there will be something under the tree for you as well."

A few days later I was wrapping gifts that some of the nurses had provided for our area families, setting them under a small tree. As I set Helen's packages in the stack, I could have sworn I heard a voice.

"Give her the candle."

No one else was in the room, but I know what I heard, and I felt an overwhelming urge to comply. I went to my desk where the two candles sat and selected the first candle, the one I'd ordered. It was nice enough.

However, I couldn't shake the admonition in my heart. This had been God's prompting, and he meant the other candle. I hemmed and hawed. I liked that candle so much . . . But I couldn't deny the instruction —it had to be the prettier one. Before I could change my mind again, I returned to the desk, grabbed the sparkling candle, and started wrapping it.

"Mom, what are you doing?" Tammi came in the room, open-mouthed and wide-eyed. "That's your favorite!"

"I know, but it was never actually mine to begin with." My words astonished even me. "I just think Miss Helen would really enjoy this."

The gifts were delivered just before Christmas, and I didn't give the candle, or Helen, a thought as I celebrated Christmas and New Year's Day with my family.

A few weeks later, Helen came to the office and walked straight to my desk.

"Hi Helen." I motioned her to a chair. She smiled—something I'd never seen her do. "How can I help you?"

"I just want to thank you, Ma'am, for saving my life."

Something different glistened through her tear-filled eyes. I walked around my desk to the front and sat on the edge.

"I don't understand."

"Well, you see . . . I was going to kill myself on Christmas Eve." Helen fished through her pocket and brought out a well-used tissue. "It's just so hard, you know? I knew I'd never be able to provide everything my boys needed." She fumbled with the damp wad, so I reached over and pulled a fresh box from my desk while she continued.

"I had all the pills laid out on the table, when I saw the gifts under the tree." She accepted a tissue and dabbed at her eyes. "I figured I should at least look at them. Then you'd know I received them. The first gift I opened was your candle and I—"

She started crying anew, her body shaking with such intensity that I walked over to console her, bringing a box of fresh tissue.

"Ma'am, I've seen you with that candle." She continued, almost in a whisper. "I was in the lobby when people offered to buy that and you *wouldn't sell it. I was in the lobby when your daughter asked for it and you said it was too precious even to give to her."*

She gazed at me, her eyes wide with wonder.

"You loved that candle, but you gave it to me. To me, Ma'am. It's..." She dabbed at the tears again. "It's the first time I've ever felt loved. I thought of my boys and how much I love them. I can't give them stuff, you know? But I can love them better than anybody else."

Helen grabbed my hands. "I threw the pills away and decided that if you cared enough about me to give me something this precious to you, then perhaps I can hang on a bit longer."

I recognized this new look I saw in her eyes. It was hope. And joy. I gave her a long hug and set back, taking her hands once again.

Helen, I do love you, and I do care about you. However, the love you're feeling is the love of Jesus Christ. He can help you, even when the world seems at its darkest. I think he wanted me to give you that candle so you could see him. If you want to learn more about Jesus, I can help you."

Before long, I had arranged to meet Helen in church the following Sunday. I saw her to the door and gave her another hug before she left.

One afternoon as I pondered the incredible changes in Helen's life, a strange fear welled up when I realized how easily this event could have ended differently. What if I hadn't listened? What if I'd been selfish and kept that candle for myself? I had no idea Helen had been in the lobby listening. I would have heard she'd taken her life and thought it sad, but I would have had no idea of my role in that until I stood before the Lord and he told me the result of my disobedience.

I vowed that whenever I believe the Lord is prompting me to do something, I will do it, regardless of how much sense it makes. Who knows how many lives it will impact? Helen may have been the target of that kindness, and she did eventually find Jesus and start pulling her life together, but I received just as much joy as she did, and perhaps more.

Since then, I've never doubted that God is in charge of my life.

WEST VIRGINIA

    Regardless of where we lived, the big white farmhouse in Webster County was always home. Grandpa Harrison built it with his own two hands and moved the family in when Mom was still a toddler. She raised each of us there, except for those few years we stayed in Maryland. The house sat at the base of a high, spacious hill, and we spent many hours sitting together on the huge family porch out front, looking out past the big ol' maple tree to the world around us.
    Grandma and Grandpa Harrison came from a simpler time, when people openly and confidently used the Bible to steer them through life. Grandpa, who died before I came along, was renowned for his generosity to the poor. I grew up listening to stories about him loading up a wagon with food from our cellar and driving it out to a needy family he'd heard about, no matter how far away they lived. Considering the high poverty rate in Webster County, this must have kept him quite busy. He and Grandma also fed anyone who came to the house, and they opened their home at night to those who needed a place to sleep. Sometimes when they got up in the mornings they had to count heads to know how many to expect for breakfast. Of course, that was

also a time when people believed in working for their food, and those passing through would often do odd jobs around the farm for Grandpa to repay him.

Grandma kept the home running, and rarely allowed her hands to sit idle. I remember watching her sewing on the old Singer, her foot pumping rhythmically on the big iron pedal and her fingers guiding material with precision as it passed under the racing needle. Sewing looked like tedious work to me, and I had no desire to learn. I'm sure my attitude at the time made God chuckle; he knew I had more than a little sewing work coming my way.

The farm itself, although no longer used for crops by the time I entered the picture, encompassed a large garden out back that filled our larder each fall. The rest of its 21 acres comprised mostly woodlands and streams—a child's paradise with plenty of places to explore.

I particularly enjoyed the enormous pine grove near our house. Within its magical walls I could play for hours or just enjoy the solitude, often making my way to a clearing at its center, where the pine-needle floor made an invitingly soft bed and the scent of Christmas stayed in the air year-round. In the summers, we'd arrange tons of needles in a path down the hill and take turns sliding to the bottom along the slick, rust-colored channel. In the winter, we flew down the same hill on our sleds.

Dad had a little workshop behind the farmhouse, where he designed and crafted beautiful artwork. I loved to sit in there and watch him cut and sand the wooden pieces and paint them so beautifully. Once he built a little green playhouse with flower boxes for Tammi and me. He also built Mitch a club house, which we girls eventually took over. His talents weren't confined to the workshop, either; he added an artful flair to everything, even to our pancakes, which he shaped into ducks and bunnies.

Although I enjoyed playing with Tammi, I hung out with Mitch whenever I could. I adored my brother, despite our seven-year age difference, and perhaps because of it. I followed him around like a puppy. When we wrestled, which was often, he called me Honeybear. And he got me to call him Wildcat, after his school mascot. Mitch had Dad's artistic flair, and I loved to watch him paint or listen while he played his guitar. He played quite well.

The farmhouse served as the Harrison family hub. All my aunts, uncles, and cousins from Mom's side lived nearby, and our place could easily accommodate a large crowd. In the winters, the Harrisons would convene on the hill for family sleigh riding parties that wound around the property and ended at Dad's workshop, where we'd huddle around the blazing hot wood stove, sipping soup and cocoa Mom had left there.

On Sundays, the same crowd assembled at the farmhouse after church for dinner. Of course, church always came first. *Obey the Lord, serve the Lord*—I'd heard it from my earliest days. Worship and prayer formed the foundation of my upbringing. In fact, as far back as I can remember, Grandma and Mom prayed for me, which I didn't appreciate at the time. However, I do believe now that their prayers protected me and kept me yearning for God in those dark years when I became so angry I couldn't speak to him.

My safe, predictable life started changing when I turned 11. That year was tough. To begin with, Dad moved back to Maryland alone. He simply couldn't find work in West Virginia at the time, so he joined his brothers (the Berkenkemper side of the family), painting buildings and rooms for a construction company. Most of the Berkenkempers lived in and near Essex, but one brother owned property in Ocean City, which is where we spent our vacation each summer.

I missed Dad terribly while he was away, but he visited often, and it sure beat leaving Webster County.

In that same year, Mitch and I were in a car accident. We probably shouldn't have been on the roads, considering the heavy snowfall that day, but Mom had the flu and needed some items from the store. She sent Mitch, by then 18, and I jumped into the passenger seat of his little Ford Pinto. We rode unbuckled, a common practice in those years before seat-belt laws. As we headed home with our goods, Mitch slowed to stay on the narrow lane that had been plowed down the middle of the road. I had just glimpsed our farmhouse in the valley below when we came face-to-face with a truck stopped in the road. Mitch veered into the snow to drive around, unaware of the patch of solid ice beneath it.

The Pinto slid across the ice, slamming hood-first into the truck, and my body crumpled. The impact from my shoulders broke the dashboard, my head cracked the windshield, and my knees dented the glove compartment. My case would have made a compelling argument for anyone trying to get those seat belt laws passed.

At first, I didn't realize the extent of my injuries. In my shock, I actually got out of the car and ran down the hill to the house screaming, "We had an accident! Mom, Mom! We had an accident!"

Then I collapsed on the couch, unable to take full breaths.

As it turned out, I had a serious neck injury that caused my throat to swell and closed off my airway. Mom stayed level-headed despite the effects of her flu and the medication she'd taken. She managed to get back up the hill to the accident site to Mitch, who had a cut on his head but was mostly dazed. He kept apologizing, particularly when he reached the house and saw me. His sorrowful face nearly broke my heart.

Mom raced me to the hospital, but was too sick to accompany me. When I later expressed my regret that she hadn't come in, she said, "God had me right where he needed me." Apparently, Mitch had been so upset about hurting me that he would have been frantic home alone.

When I think back on those next days of extreme pain and fear, I remember wondering if I would die. To an 11-year-old with a heightened imagination, the situation felt dire. The doctor could relieve the swelling in my throat with ice packs, but then the cold would somehow constrict my breathing. He assigned a nurse to sit by my side, putting ice against my throat until the airways closed, then removing the ice until the swelling re-surged. She sat there for hours.

In the darkest moments, particularly in the middle of the night, when fear set in, I prayed. "Please, God, help me get better soon. And tell Mitch I'll be okay. . . I will, won't I?"

Eventually my injuries did heal, and I bounced back with hardly a scratch.

"Just goes to show," Mom said, "God has a great purpose for your life. He must have, because Satan sure keeps trying to take you out."

Naturally, I believed her. I only had to look around to realize the extent of my blessings. Mom's candle story, which she told often, reminded me that worse things could happen than to be lying injured in the hospital. Some of the children at my school were so quiet, I found myself wondering if they were hungry, or if they suffered beatings like Sophia had back in Maryland. The image of her pleading with us not to let her mother take her still haunted me. I wondered constantly what had happened to her.

On the up-side for that year, the moment I stepped back into Mrs. Trimble's classroom Chris and I resumed our friendship and then some. Eventually we became inseparable, and people knew that if you invite Cathy to an event, you're going to get Chris, and vice versa. We were a package deal, you might say.

I loved school, not only because Chris made it fun, but because school work came relatively easy to me. I put every ounce of energy I had into it. Much of that work ethic came from Mom, who made it clear to each of us from the earliest days of our childhoods that she expected us to succeed. She reminded us repeatedly that getting good grades and a solid education would make a difference in our lives. One day Mitch informed her with a straight face that he'd been thinking about driving a trash truck for a living.

"That's fine." Mom didn't bat an eye. "There's nothing wrong with that, but make sure you have a college education so that when the time comes, you're a garbage man because it's what you want to do, not because it's your only option."

In the fall, Mitch left for Potomac State, capping off my 11th year with what felt like a kick in the gut. I missed him so much it actually hurt. He must have anticipated how difficult it would be for me to deal with his departure, because he left me with a cassette he'd recorded of him playing my favorite songs. It eased my pain a bit. On my worst days of missing him, I would trundle a small cassette player into my pine-grove hideaway and lie there, listening to him for hours. Mitch married Andrea during his college years, so he never really came home again.

I immersed myself deeper into my school work, determined to excel at the one area of my life I had some measure of control over. Chris shared my penchant for overachieving, so we made the perfect team when it came to projects, some of which we'd work on well into the night, just to make sure we handed in our best work.

We put weeks of late nights into our Social Studies Fair project on endangered species. Rather than cut out pictures of the featured animals, we hand-drew each one and placed them in habitats against a construction paper blue-sky backdrop. The display was enormous (attesting, yet again, to the incredible versatility of a rescued refrigerator box). Our diligence and flair paid off when we took first place, earning a slot at the state-wide competition.

The night before the competition, we worked for hours, redrawing animals that weren't exactly perfect and shoring up pieces to ensure they'd all stay put during the bus ride to Charleston.

The next morning, as we neared the bus and prepared to board, we each realized at the same moment that we were in trouble. Our giant display would never fit through that bus door! I would have laughed at Chris's shocked expression if I hadn't been panicking myself.

Chris's dad, a man of action and little patience for drama, whipped out his pocket knife and swiftly sliced a jagged line through the blue papered cardboard, separating the board into two pieces. Chris and I could only watch in horror as he flipped the two sections onto the bus and then motioned us aboard. We made it through the competition—apparently our dilemma was not unique because the event staff came armed with plenty of tape—and we even took a gold medal.

This incident and a few others provided me with a small glimpse of an awkward father-son relationship. Don't get me wrong, Chris had a great dad, but they struggled at times, primarily because Chris was sandwiched in the sibling lineup between two athletic brothers who more closely fit his dad's expectations as to what a son should be. Chris, who had an issue with his lungs that occasionally impeded his breathing, couldn't have competed with his brothers if he'd wanted to, which he certainly did not.

The photos on his dad's wall in the newspaper office chronicled the athletic achievements of two boys over the years, each holding different trophies as they grew, but the one picture of Chris showed a boy, perpetually 11, clutching that dreaded basketball the last year he'd played.

I remember the exact day Chris decided he'd had enough basketball. It was a week before the season opener. Chris had been going to practice regularly, hating every minute of it, of course. Hoping to cheer him up, I went outside to wait for him that afternoon around the time I knew he'd be coming to visit. As he approached, shoulders hunched and dragging his toes along the snow-covered path, pity flowed through me. He walked right to a patch of snow by my porch and plopped himself down. Lying on his back, he opened his coat and began piling snow onto his chest.

"What are you doing? You'll catch pneumonia!"

"I hope I do." He opened his mouth and sucked in the air. "Then I can't play next week."

I sat in the snow beside him.

"You know, if you get sick, you'll also miss school."

He pondered this silently before muttering, "So? I can make it up."

"Maybe, but your grades will probably go down. Besides, if you're not there, I'll have to work alone."

He looked at me, and I could see the wheels turning behind those darkening, pain-filled eyes. Finally, arriving at some resolution, he stood, shook off the snow and zipped his coat. We never really talked about what went on that night when he went home, but he didn't play ball again after that.

However, he excelled at school. When we graduated eighth grade, Chris and I shared the Valedictorian title and I received student of the year honors for the second time.

Even out of school, Chris and I were a team. We spent most of our summers at his family's camp by the river, hiking, biking, paddling his canoe down the river to the small store for sweets, or watching scary movies at each other's houses. I was as welcome in his home as he was in mine. We talked occasionally about the future…about the large house we'd buy—so big we'd have to call long-distance to speak to someone at the other end—and even agreed that our first child would be named Andrew.

Oddly though, we never dated. I didn't question it; in fact, I felt peace with this, thinking that perhaps dating would ruin what we had, which was so much more than friendship. I dated Steve for a bit, but never seriously. Even when we went to dances together, he knew I'd wind up at Chris's table at some point and would likely leave with Chris at the end of the night. Like the rest of the town, Steve had long-since accepted that Chris and I were a package deal.

I pursued success with increasing obsession in high school. I twice made the list for Who's Who Among American High School Students, made National Honor Society, earned national awards in speech and drama, and maintained a 4.0 grade-point average. To me, success was a process of checking off accomplishments on a list of milestones: obtain a good education, put degrees on my wall, earn a large salary, establish a respected position in the community, and then continue to meet any other expectations society dictated.

Although much of my drive came from Mom, I needed only to look at the town around me to see how education, or a lack of one, could affect one's lifestyle.

I felt particularly sad for Bobby, who had been in Webster Springs for as long as I could remember. Bobby, a poor and uneducated man, had nothing but a smile to offer society, and he took that seriously. Despite his shortcomings, he "worked" for his Welfare check as best he could by standing at the town's only stoplight waving at passersby, day after day. Bobby never begged. People gave him money on occasion, and they brought food to his run-down home, but not because he asked.

Some of the townspeople had called Bobby's dad Chinaman. I don't know if he was even Chinese, but he looked Asian and shuffled when he walked. Mom said he had always been part of Webster Springs for her, just as Bobby was for me. When Chinaman passed away, Bobby inherited his small shack in the crook of a curve at the bottom of a steep hill, a place that was difficult to drive to and offered no parking. Church volunteers delivering gift baskets at Christmas time had to park up the hill about a quarter-mile away and walk down to his place.

Like many of Webster's poor, Bobby was an alcoholic. He married a woman who quickly left him, whether because of the alcohol or the dismal conditions in his shack, we'll never know. However, he convinced his adult step-daughter, Sissy, to stay behind with him. She soon took up a post beside him at the stoplight, waving from morning to night.

I wondered about Bobby and Sissy from time to time. Their plight fueled compassion in my heart, but it also reminded me that I had to work hard to succeed.

Just before my senior year, I moved back to Maryland with my family. Career-focused even then, I intended to enroll in a fine arts program in Maryland after graduation, so we all moved out there a year to establish residency. I could never have afforded out-of-state tuition.

Chris and I said tearful good-byes this time, at his dad's newspaper office. He gave me a hand-drawn card of a man saying "Don't ever forget me," and I sobbed openly. This was nothing like the fourth grade parting. This time, my heart broke. I felt as if I were leaving half of me behind.

Even with the upheaval of changing schools and losing my best friend, I maintained near-perfect grades, primarily out of fear. My success of previous years in Webster Springs haunted me to the point of overwhelming. I should have felt confident because I'd been awarded Student of the Year, but instead I feared I wouldn't be able to top it. I just kept checking boxes, continuously afraid to fail. On the up-side, I met Missy, who became my surrogate best friend in Maryland, but still I missed Chris greatly.

Sometime in my senior year, I started obsessing about a piece of Mom's advice that I'd taken a bit too literally: a reminder that our actions are always observed. When I was alone I could hear her words in my head, "You can hide what you're doing from me and you can hide it from others, but you can't hide it from God." When I was with friends, her voice reminded me, "You may be the only Bible some people ever read."

Somewhere along the way, my subconscious decided I had little recourse other than to strive for perfection. At one point, I told Mom it felt like I was walking a tight rope.

"Everyone is watching me. If I'm the only Bible they're reading and I slip and fall, others will fall with me.

"Well, they shouldn't be following you," Mom said. "They need to follow God."

Still, I worried.

In a high school environment, striving for perfection translates to being no fun, so I had few friends and rarely went out. My efforts paid off when I graduated class valedictorian. Even after high school, while attending community college, I commuted from home and never partied or drank. Although I attained high marks in school, the pressure to succeed sometimes overwhelmed me. I saved a poem I wrote from that time that pretty much summed up my world view:

I'm spinning round and round
My knees they hit the ground
I can't hear a sound
There is silence
I built a wall so strong
It is for miles long
I don't know what is wrong
No one can get around it
I can't get out
No one else can get in
I won't lose
But I sure as hell won't win
The bricks get bigger on top of the wall
The foundation is crumbling but the wall won't fall
I'm spinning round and round
My knees they hit the ground
I can't hear a sound
There is silence.

At one point, I tried to snap, but God wouldn't let me. Instead, he made it clear to me, in a manner similar to Mom's candle incident, that he can and will communicate with me, but if I want to hear him, I must be prepared to listen.

It all started one night when I decided to go with the flow, so to speak. Being the good girl just got to me, I suppose. I became frustrated, spending night after night at home studying while my friends enjoyed themselves. So when Missy called to ask if I wanted to go to a party with her, I surprised us both by saying yes.

Before we left, I told Mom I'd be staying the night with Missy, unsure how events would turn out, but not wanting her to worry. I picked Missy up in my car and she navigated us to the party.

When we arrived, Missy melted into the crowd, leaving me alone amid the pounding music and swaying bodies. I made my way to the ice chest and grabbed a beer, noting the raised eyebrows around me.

"I didn't know you drank, Cathy."

"Wow, are you sure you want that? I can bring you a Coke…"

"Cathy, you know that's beer, right?"

Frustrated by their attention, I made a beeline for an out-of-the-way corner and sat, surrounded by people drinking and laughing, people who knew how to enjoy themselves. Yet, I just watched, holding my unopened beer.

"Cathy! What are you doing?" Rob, a friend from one of my art classes, had come into the room and stopped short when he spotted me. "You don't drink. Give me that."

He snatched the beer from my hands and walked away.

Dumbfounded and somewhat embarrassed, I felt the blood rise beneath my collar.

If I want to drink, who's to say I can't?

I forgot all about Missy and stormed out of the house. I jumped in the car and drove to my friend Paul's home so I could vent to him.

While whining to Paul about people not letting me drink if I wanted to, I managed to talk myself into going back out to finish what I'd started. In Paul's defense, he did try to keep me from leaving.

I returned to the party and looked for Missy, who had apparently left with someone else.

This night is not going anything like I imagined.

Frustrated and angry, I grabbed two bottles of beer from the cooler and returned to my car, tossing them on the passenger's seat. By then it was one in the morning, and I'd told Mom I wouldn't be home. I had no idea what to do next, so I just drove onto the main road, fuming.

Why is everyone trying to run my life? If I want to drink, I'm gonna drink, and that's that!

"No, you're not!"

I nearly drove off the road. Whether the words were in my head or not, I couldn't say, but the voice rang out so loud and clear, I could have sworn it came from someone speaking beside me. Despite being startled, I vented my anger at the air.

"Yes, I will."

"You won't."

If anyone had seen me at that moment, they would have thought me nuts, driving down the road arguing. We kept up our "discussion" until I came to a church parking lot and turned in. The serene glow cast by the illuminated steeple did little to appease my anger.

From the Remnants

I grabbed a bottle but couldn't pry its lid off. Frustrated, I tried the second, which wouldn't budge either. Again I snarled at my invisible passenger.

"Back off! First my mother, then my friends, and now you…what are you, an angel?" But I knew it was God. "Why won't anyone let me do what I want?"

I opened the car door and fumbled again with the beer cap. It practically slid right off. Now thoroughly chastised, I poured the contents on the ground and dropped the bottle in the gravel. I did the same with the second.

"I hope you're happy." I started to close the car door when the voice spoke again.

"Pick them up."

"Really? I can't even litter?"

"Pick them up."

I snatched up the bottles and threw them onto the floor of my car. No longer concerned about what Mom would think, I drove home and tried to sneak in, but she caught me. I threw the bottles onto the table.

I suddenly missed Grandma and Webster. I didn't belong in Maryland. "I want to go home!" I left Mom staring at the bottles and ran to my bedroom.

The next morning unfettered by the previous night's pretense, I told Mom what had happened. Her response surprised me, but it shouldn't have.

"Well now, that makes sense." She smiled as she sipped her coffee. "I wondered what was going on, so I prayed for you last night. I knew you weren't going to get into trouble because I asked God to surround you with his angels and keep you from making mistakes. Now I know why, I guess."

My mind flashed to an earlier time, when Mom had started praying for Mitch out of the blue. Later, he told her he'd been at a night club. In the midst of partying, his eyes had opened suddenly, and he'd been able to clearly see the destructive paths of those around him, understanding at once that he had to get out of there.

I'd say there aren't many weapons more powerful than a Mama's prayer.

TORN

Sophia Arnett

It couldn't be...

My hand hovered over the time cards as I noticed the typed letters of the name above mine.

It's an unusual name. What are the chances?

Trembling, I lowered my hand and turned around, almost afraid to hope. But there she stood, my Sophia, grown now, glowing with health and grinning from ear to ear.

"I wondered if you'd recognize me." She leapt forward and we hugged each other tightly. "When I saw your name go on the board yesterday I just knew it had to be you."

A wave of joy and relief rushed over me. She'd made it! I had a thousand questions, but they would have to wait. This was my first day at the restaurant and I had to clock in.

"Sophia, if you only knew how many times I've thought of you. Wondered how you're doing…When can we get together?"

A hint of sadness clouded her cheerful face. She pulled her time card from the rack and clocked out.

From the Remnants

"Oh, Cathy, we can't. This is my last day here." Then she brightened. "I've been accepted at the police academy, and I'm leaving today. I'll be specializing in child abuse cases. You know, because of my background. I figure I can ask the right questions because I've been there...and I'll know what to look for."

Then, as quickly as she'd re-entered my life, Sophia was gone again. I never saw her after that day, but my heart felt peace when I thought of her. To this day I believe God orchestrated this special meeting just for me, to show me he had heard and answered my years of prayers for Sophia.

I learned something else from Sophia's story as well. At the time, I wasn't in the habit of connecting the dots between events in our lives and God's provision, but I've since come to understand that although Sophia's abusive childhood hadn't come from God, he did help her find a way to use it for good. Wherever Sophia is today, I'm certain she's bringing light and hope into children's lives.

Throughout my years in Maryland, I called Chris whenever I could. He had enrolled in Marshall University in Huntington. Sometimes, if I called and he was out, I'd talk to his roommate, Brian. We struck up a pretty good over-the-wire friendship.

I settled into a routine at Essex Community College, still commuting from my parents' home nearby. After graduating with an Associate's degree, I enrolled at Towson State University to study Fine Arts. Around this time, I struck up a relationship with a man in the apartment complex where I lived. We dated for approximately two years when I discovered he was gambling and taking drugs behind my back, so that ended rather abruptly.

Then I met David, who worked day shift in the maintenance department at Golden Ring Mall where I freelanced in the evenings creating publicity artwork. (I also had a job as a graphic artist with the Maryland Paperbox Company.) In the days leading up to Christmas, I took an assignment constructing huge Santa frames to hold posters throughout the mall. The work wasn't difficult, but time-consuming. When a last-minute rush job came through, David volunteered to stay one evening to help me make my deadline.

David didn't drink, smoke, or do drugs, which put him in high standing with me from the start. He was also a church-going, hard-working, divorced man, sharing joint custody of his daughter, Christina. I liked him, and we soon started dating.

When David asked me to marry him, I realized it could be a solution to my high-speed life. If I were married, I could let my guard down a bit—stop trying to be perfect and watching what I said and did all of the time. I said yes.

I may have loved him but I'm not sure I knew how to love at the time. On a visit home I saw Chris and we talked about the wedding.

"Are you happy Cathy?" His blue eyes peered into my own from beneath his John Denver-like crop.

"Yes, Chris. I think I am."

"Well then, so am I." Chris gave me a long hug and assured me I could still call any time.

"I mean that, Cath. Day or night."

I smiled and turned away.

David and I married on April 21, 1990 at a sunrise beach service in Ocean City. Audrey, my friend and supervisor at the paper company, stood as my Maid of Honor.

We moved into a townhouse just two blocks from his brother, Duane and his wife Vada, and we tried to expand our family.

I could think of no greater joy than to have a child, so when we learned I'd become pregnant, I looked delightfully forward to the journey ahead. I hummed through my days, picking out decorations for the nursery and buying tiny clothes for my new baby.

Near the third month of pregnancy, I began to feel excruciating pain and discomfort. The doctors identified the cause as extremely elevated hormone levels, and thought I might be carrying twins.

When I started bleeding heavily in my fifth month, the doctors thought one of the twins might have died. During an examination they determined I had only one, healthy baby. They stopped the bleeding and sent me home. Relieved, I let myself dream about who my baby would be, and what kind of parents David and I would be. I smiled constantly, thinking about the joy that waited ahead.

Within a few days David again rushed me to Johns Hopkins Hospital. There, four months ahead of schedule, Tiffany came into the world, tiny, fragile, and broken.

I knew she was in trouble even before the doctor spoke.

"David and Cathy, you have a decision to make." The doctor's voice was calm, but I didn't want to hear what he had to say.

David took my hand.

"Your daughter's lungs are not developed, her brain is not developed, and she has many other debilitating problems. We can put her on life support, but you should know, there is a possibility that she may never come off of it."

Stunned, I could think only of Terry, now in her 30s and still living life from a 4-month-old's perspective. Could I watch my little girl go through the same thing? I think now, with hind-sight, that if Terry hadn't been part of my childhood, I wouldn't have been able to let Tiffany go. Instead, I had a clear picture of what I would be saying yes to. I knew that even if the machines did prolong her life, she would never get a chance to truly live. David and I tearfully opted not to put her on life support. It was, and still is, the most horrible decision I've ever had to make.

The nursing staff at John Hopkins treated us with tender compassion. They left us alone with Tiffany, but checked on me often, and they explained the situation to Mom and Tammi when they arrived. I spent the next hour holding my precious daughter, watching her little chest rise and fall as she struggled to breathe. Such a surreal, pure, and painfully sad time, just waiting for her heart to stop beating.

"I don't know how long we have, sweet girl." I murmured against her soft head as tears dropped from my cheeks onto hers. "But I promise I will hold you for your entire life."

And as I held her, Tiffany's tiny heart beat one last time, and she went on to Heaven.

I sat with her, crying, until a nurse took her from me. I asked that someone call the funeral home, which surprised some people. I couldn't conceive not having a funeral, but even the funeral home staff commented that they'd never picked up such a tiny baby.

David grieved deeply, and then somehow pulled himself together. He saw that it wasn't as simple for me, and he tried his best to help me "get over it," but that wasn't going to happen.

When we left the hospital, Mom and Tammi rushed ahead to the house to clear the nursery, taking down all the toys and decorations I'd put up over the months. It didn't help. I couldn't walk into that room and not know it was supposed to be for Tiffany.

I began the day of Tiffany's funeral service in a panic when I realized we hadn't dressed her.

She just has to be dressed!

I called the funeral home and asked them not to seal the casket, then I raced to a store and picked out a newborn shirt with pink rosebuds and a small guardian angel pin. I brought the items to the funeral home, where Tiffany and I spent our final moments alone.

Balancing her miniature white casket on my lap, I gently slipped the shirt over her head and put her arms into the sleeves. Her sweet little finger wrapped around mine and I almost fell apart, but the experience gave me one more precious memory that I'll treasure forever. The shirt looked like a dress on her, and the pin on her collar seemed huge for such a tiny angel.

David entered with Christina, who was holding a small stuffed lamb. I let her put the lamb into the casket, and we added a pink carnation before closing the lid. The three of us were the only people at her service, as we'd requested.

This is where my battle against darkness began.

ҳ ҳ ҳ ҳ ҳ ҳ

"Oh, Chris, it just hurts so much!"

I held the phone to my wet cheeks, longing to be back in Webster Springs.

"I know Cath. I know." Chris's soothing voice sent a sliver of comfort through the line. "How's David holding up?"

"That's part of the problem." I sniffed. "He's fine. Just fine. He's started back working on the new house like nothing's wrong, but I can't get there. I think I'm driving him nuts with all my crying, but I just can't stop."

"Shhh. I know it's hard, and you can call me any time you need to talk, but at some point you have to look forward. If it helps, find something distracting to do, something you can focus on to give your mind a rest."

From the Remnants

I tried. I stared at wallpaper samples for the new house as if my life depended on it, but the colors reminded me of Tiffany—specifically the pinks. More often than not, all thoughts came full-circle back to Tiffany.

The weeks and months took their toll on my emotions and on our marriage. One small bit of closure came with the hospital report a few weeks after I returned home. Although I'd refused the hospital's request to perform an autopsy, they did run some tests on Tiffany's placenta and determined that she'd had Trisomy 18, also known as Edwards Syndrome, which is a common cause of prenatal deaths. Only 10 percent of children with T18 survive to their first birthday, and even then, are usually wrought with medical complications. Little Tiffany had been spared a difficult fight, and I'll always consider that God's blessing.

But knowing the cause of her death didn't make up for the anger I felt toward God. I couldn't understand why he would put us through all that. As the weeks passed, although David tried to show patience with me, my sadness darkened to the point where he couldn't get into my heart. Not even Mom or Tammi could understand my anguish, as miscarriages were common in our family. Truth be told, *I'm* not even sure why I couldn't "get over it," as David suggested. I became lost in my sorrow.

David threw all his energy into designing our new home, which he was constructing on 3.5 acres of land he'd acquired during his first marriage. The large, flat lot contained many beautiful fruit trees and promised to support a lovely home. He handled the business details with the contractors, electricians, and plumbers, and he stayed busy obtaining permits and supervising construction.

He tried to help me submerge myself into the project as well, visually painting a picture for me of the three-bedroom brick rancher we were building, with its lovely fireplace in the living room and spacious dining and kitchen areas.

Truthfully, I should have been able to set aside my sorrows, with just the busy-ness of life. In addition to house planning and decorating, I continued my freelance work at the mall and my job at the paper company, and I tried to continue work on my degree. I just couldn't seem to shake the debilitating sadness.

I learned not to break down in front of David if I could help it. I sensed his frustration at not being able to make everything better. How helpless he must have felt. We shared some good times, but for the most part, my misery eclipsed every light moment.

When I learned I was pregnant again, the prospect of a second chance at motherhood brought great hope and excitement, but also fear. I researched Trisomy 18 with a fervor worthy of a gifted academic, and learned enough to know I did nothing wrong and could not have prevented Tiffany's death. The doctors assured me that my baby would be okay, explaining that trisomies are random occurrences and unlikely to occur twice in the same family, particularly for someone still so young. All medical visits and tests showed progress, with no complications. My doctor pronounced it a perfect pregnancy.

In mid-April my Aunt Ruthie, who had been battling lung cancer, went into the hospital. Ruth, one of Mom's four sisters, was a sweetheart. She spoke softly and pampered everyone. When she had developed lung cancer five years earlier, the doctors removed one of her lungs and told us that if she made it through five years without the cancer returning then she'd be okay. In the fifth year, it returned.

Now she had only days to live. The doctors placed her on oxygen and gave her medication to make her as comfortable as possible, but she'd lost nearly all awareness of who we were and there was nothing anyone could do but sit with her.

A few days later, on April 19, I went to the cemetery to put some Easter flowers on Tiffany's grave. I walked among the headstones, taking notice of the smaller markers.

So many mothers without their children.

Near Tiffany's grave I spotted two little headstones side-by-side—brothers, judging from the names etched on them.

That poor mother. I can't imagine being in her shoes. My one loss about killed me. How could anyone endure two?

I laid Tiffany's flowers at her marker and stood there. My attempt to pray ended, as usual, with tearful questions directed toward this supposedly good God. Even after all these months, I still couldn't make sense of his decision, but I knew he had her, and that helped, some.

From the Remnants

With my hand resting on my belly, I considered the plight of the mother, and felt grateful for this new life, and new hope growing within me.

April 22nd started as a good day. David and I had celebrated our third anniversary the night before, and I felt hopeful as I went in for my doctor's appointment. My baby was 15 weeks along and doing well. The sonogram showed no problems, the tiny heart beat strongly, and the doctor was pleased.

I spent the day at home, washing laundry and taking care of small chores. I noticed my trousers were slightly damp, but I felt no pain. I figured the baby had found a way to press against my bladder.

The dampness persisted throughout the day, and by evening, I started to worry. Trying to remain calm, I picked up my keys and headed for the door, pausing to give David and Christina kisses while they watched television on the couch.

"I'm heading over to the hospital to get something checked out." My voice sounded forced, even to me.

"Do you want me to come with you?" David looked at Christina and I could tell he was trying to decide who he could call to look after her.

"No, I'll be fine. My visit today went well. I'm just being a little paranoid, I'm sure. I should be back soon."

At the hospital, the doctor gave me a quick exam and then she stood, looking over my head toward the door.

"Cathy, is there anyone here with you?" The tenderness in her eyes made my heart lurch.

"No, I drove myself . . . Why? What's wrong?"

She hesitated, then took a deep breath before she spoke.

"Hon, your water's ruptured; you're fully dilated."

No, no, no, no. This isn't happening.

"I'm so sorry. The baby's gone. There's nothing I can do."

What remained of my world came crashing down around me, and a picture from the cemetery I'd visited flashed before my eyes.

Oh, no, I'm in her shoes! I'll have two headstones now!

Turmoil erupted, but I could barely take in anything that was happening. Someone called my husband and they told me he was on his way. I still had to deliver the child. I had to respond to questions. I just couldn't. My mind became paralyzed by that single thought:

I'm in her shoes. I'm in her shoes!

When David arrived, I was sobbing. I looked at him and cried, "I'm in her shoes!" He had no idea what I was ranting about.

They let me see my baby, a little boy we named Matthew. Such a tiny angel. His little footprint was the size of my thumbnail but he had all of his little fingers and toes. He was so perfect, I didn't want to look away. However, as I sat there, frozen in time with my son, a nurse came into my room and broke the stillness.

"Do you want to take him, or do you want me to just put him out back with the rest of them?"

Horrified and shocked, I tried to comprehend her question.

How could she even ask that?

"Of course I want him. He's going to have a proper burial, just like his sister."

The world—not mine, but all around me—resumed its normal rhythm. Nurses stepped in less frequently, and David left to take Christina to her mother's house. Alone in my room, I stared at the walls until my mind began to subliminally read the messages on the corkboard by my bed. I sobbed so hard and forcefully that nurses came running from down the hall.

"Take this down!" I cried, pointing at the baby fliers and pictures. Joyful glimpses of a world I'd never know. Sweet baby faces filled with life. "Get it out of here!"

They rushed to comply but the pictures stayed in my head. I felt as though I couldn't catch my breath.

An older nurse came to my side and took my hand.

"I know, Cathy. I know."

"How could you!" Bitterness welled within me. "Have you ever lost a child?"

"Yes, I have. Twins, in fact. Two sweet little boys I'll never know until I see them in Heaven." She spoke in a soft voice, sharing her story. "I finally found peace knowing they are with Jesus, but it takes time."

I couldn't imagine ever feeling peace again, but I just let her talk. She stayed with me, holding my hand until I finally drifted to sleep from exhaustion.

From the Remnants

Again, the funeral home staff seemed surprised at our request to have a service. This time, however, I couldn't dress my little one; his tiny body fit in one of my hands. I wrapped a man's handkerchief around him like a blanket and set him in the casket. The blue carnation I laid beside him looked enormous next to his little head.

I hadn't started decorating a nursery yet, so Mom and Tammi didn't have to rush ahead of me this time. This turned out to be a good thing, because while I tended to Matthew's burial arrangements, they were busy saying good-bye to Aunt Ruth.

Mom told me later that Ruth's remaining lung had filled with fluid and, because she was dying, nobody told her about me being in the hospital; it just made no sense to burden her. At one point, as Mom waited by her bedside, Aunt Ruth sat up and removed her oxygen mask. Despite completely lacking lung capacity, she started talking, using plain, coherent words, surprising everyone there.

"Jesus is here. Can't you see him?" Her voice rang out strong and clear. "He's waiting on me."

Ruth looked around at her family and smiled. "Don't be afraid. Heaven is more beautiful than you could ever imagine." She turned to Mom. "Don't worry, Ann and Wallace and the girls are on their way. They'll get here in time."

"Oh, Sweetie, Ann can't make it. She already called."

"She'll make it."

Ruth then spoke to the others in the room, telling them where their loved ones were on the road and promising they would all make it to her bedside to say good bye.

Then Ruth took Mom's hand and looked into her eyes.

"Tell Cathy not to worry about the baby. Jesus has him and he's doing fine." Her words took Mom by surprise, because not even I had known he was a boy until he arrived.

After she said all she had left, Ruth laid back and resumed her coma state. Just as promised, Aunt Ann arrived with her family, and were greeted with wide-eyed stares. Other family members arrived and all said their good-byes, after which Ruth took her last breath and left us.

Life returned to normal for everyone but me. The compounded grief on my heart became an anchor I just couldn't lift off, and it threatened to crush me. David, Mom, and Tammi didn't understand my prolonged anguish. Neither did I, to be frank. Again I turned my anger toward God, demanding to know why he took my babies. Why he put me through so much pain.

"It makes no sense God!" I'd scream at him in my darkest times. "If we're all born with a purpose, what was theirs? How can you tell me my children served their purpose!?

God said nothing, which didn't help. Back at home, my days filled to the brim with well-meaning people who tried to make me forget the heartache by reminding me how "good" God is.

"God is love."

"God loves you."

"He's a good God."

"Everything good comes from God."

I simply couldn't believe them anymore. I told God so, many times.

"You can't *possibly* be a good God." I'd scream at him. "If you are, why did this happen?"

Deep down, my heart knew I needed to worship God despite my sadness. However, I couldn't bear to give him any type of praise whatsoever, only questions.

. . . Which God never answered.

The well-meaning people continued laying on the kind words, which only compounded my anger:

"Don't worry, sweetie. You're young, and you can have more."

"Everything happens for a reason."

"They're in a better place."

Every word pierced my heart like a dagger. Most times, I could only stare back in disbelief, unable to fathom how they could be so flippant over something so big. Other times I'd snap at them and leave the room, usually crying.

One of the worst conversations I had during this time was with Duane, my brother-in-law. I remember him coming into my kitchen one morning while I sat at the table, feeling lost.

"Mornin' Sis, got any coffee in that pot?" Duane grinned as he poked his head through the door.

I dabbed my eyes with my sleeve and shoved my wad of damp tissue into my pocket before I looked up, but it didn't matter.

"What's wrong?" He set his keys on the counter and rushed to hug me.

So tired of that question.

"What's usually wrong?" I yanked free and went to the cupboard to pull out a mug.

Duane placed his hands on my shoulders, turning me so I had to look at him.

"Cathy, it's been months. You've got to move on." He looked into my eyes. "Just keep the faith. God will get you through this."

I pulled away again, fighting to keep the pot still as I filled his cup.

"Don't you dare try to talk to me about God! He took my babies and I can never forgive him for that!"

Duane sighed. We'd had this conversation many times.

"You don't know this is God's fault. Remember the story of Job? He lost his children and his home, but because he remained faithful, God gave everything back."

The more he talked, the angrier I became.

I set the coffee down and jabbed at his chest. "So you're telling me that Job had, what, 20 children?" I stepped forward, he stepped back.

"And ten of them died?"

Another step.

"And that's supposed to be a good thing?"

Another step. "A *blessing*?"

With my jabbing finger, I'd inched him backward across the floor to the kitchen door. Concern, frustration, and sadness clouded his face.

"Okay, Okay, I'm Sorry, Cathy … I'm leaving." He turned away, then stopped and looked back. "I'm worried about you."

As I closed the door, remorse prickled at my conscience. Still, I couldn't exactly drop my anger on command. I draped the anger and depression over my head like a warm blanket, shutting out the world around me. More and more frequently, David found errands away from home, warily keeping his distance. I knew I made people uncomfortable, but I couldn't let it go.

Everywhere I went, same conversation, different words. People meant well, but their comments grated on my nerves.

"God won't give you more than you can handle."

"Just give your grief to God."

"God has another angel."

Even Mom could only come up with, "Sometimes we don't know all the answers," which wasn't helpful in the least.

The more they tried to comfort me, the angrier I became. Sometimes, I wanted to punch them in the face. I wanted to scream at the top of my lungs, "Stop saying stupid stuff!"

If one more person tells me God is good, I'm going to lose my mind.

TATTERED

"Hello?"

I cradled the phone to my mouth and tried to speak, but could only manage a weak sob. The pain crushed against my heart so heavily I could barely breathe.

"Cathy? Is that you?"

I nodded into the nothingness and squeaked out another sound.

"Hang in there, Honey, I'm coming!"

Missy hung up on her end, and I did the same, dropping into a sobbing heap on the couch until the doorbell rang. I opened the door and there stood Missy in blue flannel pajamas and fuzzy slippers, clutching a pillow under her arm.

"Looks like a good night for a sleep-over." She smiled.

I melted in her arms and we went to the couch. She held me until my wracking sobs subsided, and we just sat there, watching mindless television side-by-side. She asked no questions and offered no advice. Eventually, my heart settled and my head began nodding.

"Cathy, we should really get you to bed." Missy stood, offering her hand, and I let her lead me to the bedroom. "I'll stay here until David comes."

You're so good to me.

Where my family was concerned, my grief had become tiresome. I learned to shut off my tears and keep them bottled up until I could be alone, which was often. David worked the night shift at his job and spent his days on our nearly finished home, so I had plenty of time to brood.

Fortunately, I also had many friends. Missy's willingness to come over, day or night, just to sit with me, helped immensely. Chris, too, made himself available to talk, regardless of how late I called. I wished he weren't so far away, but just hearing his calming voice sometimes gave me the strength to face another day. At other times I called strangers on the Compassionate Friends Network hotline, an encouraging organization of parents who had lost children.

But for all their support, I still felt relentlessly lost. I yearned to return to a normal life, whatever that meant.

※ ※ ※ ※ ※ ※

Something kept tugging at me to go to church.

No. I'm not ready.

Despite spending years of Sundays sitting in a church pew, listening to stories about all the great things God has done, I could no longer believe in his goodness, or in our *so-called* purpose. And prayer? Forget it. Any attempts to pray usually ended in a bitter lashing out.

"Why are you so cruel, God? Why give them to me and then take them away? Why am even I praying? It's obvious you don't care!"

However, something wouldn't let me turn my back on God completely. Seeds planted during my childhood kept nudging me, reminding me he was there, waiting patiently for me to take a step. Despite my anger, I knew I had to keep my faith, as fragile as it was, or I would never be whole again.

I mustered my strength one Sunday, about six weeks after losing Matthew, and dressed for church. Every article of clothing I put on added to the suffocating heaviness weighing on my chest. Finally, with lead feet and a seething heart, I set out.

Once at the church, I stood outside the large wooden door for what felt like hours, shaking like a leaf. It took every ounce of strength I had to open it. I steeled myself against the smiling faces and well-meaning people waiting on the other side who would overwhelm me with their questions and platitudes.

I might be able to face them, but I'm not so sure about facing God.

My shaking increased as I pushed my way through the door and into the foyer. I could walk no further, unable to bear the thought of entering the sanctuary. Standing amid this sea of smiling, joyful people, feeling hopeless, I gave up.

I can't do this!

Just as I turned around, a woman with the most peaceful face I'd ever seen stepped forward and took my hand.

"Welcome." The woman's voice sounded like peace. "Can I help you find a seat?"

On cue, the tears started trickling down my face.

"I'm sorry." I edged backward, pointing at the sanctuary. "I want to…I just can't."

She patted my hand. "That's okay. Follow me." She led me to the pastor's office. "He won't mind." She chuckled, directing me to a chair. "He's a little busy."

I smiled weakly and followed her into the room, sitting in the chair she indicated. This wonderful woman held my hand for more than an hour as I alternately wept and sat in silence. The woman asked no questions, and she voiced no opinions. When the service in the sanctuary ended, she walked me to the door and gave me a loving hug.

"We'll try again next week, okay?"

And so it began. Every week I forced myself to walk through that door, and every week someone would sit with me in the pastor's office. At least six or seven different women sat with me, sometimes in pairs or groups and sometimes one-on-one. We talked, but only if I wanted to, and we prayed together. Not once did I feel as if I were an inconvenience. Not once did anyone suggest I should just "get over it."

They held onto me when I couldn't hold on. None of the ladies at the church said anything unless I spoke first. I don't remember what any one of them looked like, and I can't remember their names. I just remember their patience, and their gentleness, and above all, what they didn't say. That silence spoke louder than any advice they could have given.

Each week I gazed hopefully at the sanctuary doors, but my mind talked me out of entering.

If you walk through those doors, they're going to tell you he's a good God. They will be praising him. Singing, raising their arms. Thanking him. Is that what you want to see?

No. I'd resolutely turn away. God didn't deserve praise.

I have nothing to thank you for, God. You've taken everything from me. You gave them to me and then snatched them away. You're not a good God. You're just plain cruel.

Although the women didn't judge me, I judged myself. I knew the path to healing was beyond those sanctuary doors. I knew my behavior matched that of a petulant child. I knew God wanted me to come back.

I've got to do this.

Finally, after weeks of struggling, one Sunday I pushed my way into the foyer and said to the kind-faced woman who met me, "I think I'm ready to go in."

The woman beamed and took my hand, and we walked together toward the music.

I made it as far as the sanctuary door. The sound of beautiful voices on the other side, singing praises to a merciful and loving God, unraveled me like a pile of discarded fishing line. I had to run away.

The next week I tried again, and every week after that.

Each time, one of the women accompanied me, and I gradually gained the emotional strength to sit just inside the door for a few minutes. I forced myself to withstand the suffocating praise music until I couldn't breathe, and then I'd run right back out. Over the weeks I'd sit a bit longer, for a few songs, then for 30 minutes, through the sermon, and finally, I made it to the end of a service.

Despite the victory, everything I heard in there angered me. When the congregation sang beautiful hymns of praise to the Lord, I mouthed the words, but I felt nothing. When the preacher spoke about God's love and tender mercies toward us, I sat, stone-faced, thinking, pretty much non-stop, "Then how could you do that to me, God?"

Whenever I sat in the sanctuary, one of the ladies positioned herself either by my side or behind me. I know now that they were praying, but at the time, their mere presence meant everything to me. I never felt like an inconvenience. It took about six months before I could actually hear the words spoken there with an open heart. I attribute everything to those nameless, faceless women, and to their steadfast obedience to the Lord's instruction to love me and care for me. They never gave up, and for that I'll always be grateful.

David and I moved into the new house in the fall. At first, caught up in the bustle and excitement of furnishing the place and decorating for Christmas, we ignored the dark cloud that loomed over our heads, but eventually, the cloud opened. We had very little to say to each other anymore. Our marriage was failing.

David tried, I know he did. But we lived in an unchanging cycle of hurt and anger. For my part, I couldn't understand how he could deal with the loss of our babies so . . . efficiently. It seemed like he'd already moved on as if nothing had happened. I stewed over what I saw as his insensitivity, fanning the flames of my frustration until I had to lash out.

"You just don't care!"

He had no answers. David, like most of my friends and family members, felt helpless around me. By then I'd been grieving more than a year and still couldn't stop crying. He wanted to "fix" me, but he couldn't.

As the holidays waned and our house settled into a post-New Year's quiet, the emotional distance between us became impossible to ignore.

I returned to work despondent after the Christmas break and poured out my story to Audrey, my supervisor. She said that one day I'd wake up and just know it was time to leave the marriage.

"When that happens, I'll have a room ready for you." She touched my shoulder. "Just let me know."

Today, with my older and wiser hind-sight, I understand that we might have turned the situation around had we sought counselling. At the time, however, the darkness of my depression had cast such a cloud of hopelessness over our lives, the thought didn't occur to either of us.

From the Remnants

One day in early January I woke before David and got out of bed, pressed by a giant emptiness. I realized I could feel nothing. I looked back from the doorway of our bedroom, surprised to see this stranger lying in our bed. I didn't even know who he was.

Over the next couple of weeks, I secretly packed boxes in my closets, accumulating the few items I wanted to keep. It wasn't long before David and I found something to argue about, and I blurted out mid-fight that I was leaving. I went into the other room and dialed Audrey's number.

"It's time."

I arrived on Audrey's doorstep clutching a teddy bear I'd grabbed from the house. For the next two weeks, that bear was rarely more than arm's reach away. I cried into its soft fur again and again as waves of sadness threatened to sweep me away.

Chris became my rock during this time, although he could only listen helplessly when I sobbed to him over the phone.

"Why, Chris? I just don't understand."

"I don't either Cath." After a brief silence he spoke again. "I guess life can be like a science fair, you know? You can do everything right, but sometimes you get the purple ribbon, and other times you get the stupid plaque."

"Oh my gosh, I haven't thought about that in years!" Despite my misery, I had to laugh, recalling the middle-school project we'd worked so hard to complete—specifically for the coveted purple ribbon that had been awarded in previous years. We'd both determined it would be ours when the time came. Our Acid Rain display took grand prize, and we'd waited so expectantly for that regal award.

"Sorry, no ribbon for you." Chris chuckled. "You get this, this, monstrosity!"

The organizers had changed the award that year, replacing the ribbon with a large, hideous, wooden plaque painted blue with the chemical symbol for gold (AU) on it in gold lettering.

"Ha! Remember how we fought over who would take it home? Neither of us wanted to be seen with it." I smiled to think of that more innocent time. "Yeah, I guess it's like that. I got the stupid plaque."

"It will be okay, Cath." Chris's voice quieted. "You'll make it through this. If you need anything, I'm here."

David knew "the drill," having been divorced before, so he hired a lawyer immediately. At 25, and still rather naïve, I had no idea I was even supposed to *get* a lawyer, nor did anyone tell me I should.

We met to review the separation papers February 5, 1993. I had no idea what I was reading. As I stared at the words on the paper, my mind whirled through a roller coaster of emotion, from sadness, thinking the failure was all my fault, to disgust, despising him so much I vowed I wouldn't take even a fork he had touched. I just wanted to disappear. I didn't care about the home, his *dream* home.

A dream I'd always thought we'd share.

I signed the paperwork, not realizing that it also awarded him all our savings, and I'd be left with nothing.

While I was staying with Audrey, the paper company landed a blow we hadn't expected. They'd lost some major contracts, forcing the company to close its doors. In addition, the new manager at the mall sent notice that he no longer needed my freelance art services, opting instead to hire a group out of Washington DC. I'd lost both my jobs at once.

I wrote to Chris saying I'd had enough, scrawling in tiny words beneath my signature, *"Help, help, help! I need to get out of here!"*

A few days later he called.

"Hang in there, Honey, we are coming to get you."

While Chris and Brian barreled down the road to Maryland in his pickup truck, his mother Karen, looked for job openings at the Mental Health Agency in Webster Springs where she was a director. They had an opening for a home-care aide. It represented the only ray of hope in an otherwise dismal outlook, so I accepted the position.

The night before I left Maryland, as I sat in the middle of my bedroom packing the last of my belongings, David came in and dropped to the floor beside me. Soon we were talking like best friends, and we shared probably the best conversation we'd had in weeks or even months. In the morning, David and I ate breakfast together. A bittersweet way to end a relationship that had started in hope and joy.

As David left for work, I walked him to the front door. We embraced and he kissed me goodbye like any normal day.

"I love you, Cathy." I knew he meant it, but I also knew that it wasn't enough.

"I love you too." Teary eyed, I watched him drive away knowing it was the last time I would see him. I sat in silence as I waited for Chris and Brian to arrive. It felt like forever.

It took almost no time to load my few belongings into Chris's truck. I returned to the house one last time and walked from room to room, saddened to think of all the dreams that would never be fulfilled there. The teddy bear I'd been clinging to for the past few weeks sat near the front door, his blank brown eyes staring at nothing, which matched my mood. I tucked him under my arm and walked outside.

As the door closed behind me, I couldn't help but wonder whether the door had also closed on the saddest chapter of my life.

Or will my sorrows just follow me?

SALVAGED

So, God, I still don't understand. What was their purpose? How could you take them before they had a chance to serve even you?

My little red Geo Prism drove practically on autopilot behind Chris and Brian in the pickup truck. Focused so completely on my sorrows, I barely noticed the majestic, white-topped Appalachian Mountains looming against the dismal gray February sky. I gave the stuffed bear on my lap yet another despairing squeeze.

. . . And why did you let me marry him God, if he wasn't the one?

I pictured David sitting in front of that beautiful fireplace, happily enjoying the house he and I had worked so long to build but would never share. House, not home. How strange, that the word 'home,' for me still seemed to be the big white farmhouse.

How could you let me lose my job knowing this was coming and I'd need the money?

I hadn't told Mom and Dad I was coming, but I simply had nowhere else to turn. They'd welcome me and my emptiness without asking too many questions.

Even so, what am I going to do now, God?

We drove for seven hours, finally pulling into my parents' driveway just as dusk settled over the farmhouse. Chris hopped down

From the Remnants

from his truck and came to my car door as I climbed out, still clutching the bear. We walked together across the snow-patched yard and up the porch stairs. The familiar glow from the porch light somehow touched my despondent heart.

And at that moment, as I stood on the porch waiting for the door to open, time stood still. My mind swirled with all the loss I'd experienced. All the nothingness of my life. All the sadness in my heart. No babies, no husband, no savings, no job, no home, no plan for the future.

I've lost absolutely everything, God. You can't fix this. Even if you could, why would you? As mad as I have been at you, I wouldn't blame you for turning your back on me.

I didn't realize at the time, but that was my defining moment. From that point on, I could have been swallowed up by self-pity, or I could have given up on life and let the world pass me by. Instead, God determined that I would survive. As I stepped across the threshold, God changed me. He picked me up and set me on a new path.

. . . perhaps, back onto the path he'd intended me to walk in the first place.

The change wasn't evident at first. I stayed with Mom and Dad for about a year while I regained my footing. I took the job as a home care aide, working at a long-term housing facility for people with disabilities. The work challenged me, physically, but it enabled me to stay in school.

Still determined to check "diploma" off my list of must-haves, I transferred my Maryland credits to Glenville State College, 90 minutes away. Most of my classes started at 8 a.m., so I worked the night shift at the facility, clocking out at 4 a.m., going home to shower and then jumping back into my car for the ride to Glenville.

I switched my major from fine arts to behavioral science. Art work, regardless of its quality, wouldn't be as profitable in the country as it had been in the city, and in this pre-internet commerce era, I had no way to market my work outside the area.

Besides, behavioral science seemed to answer a rekindled flame somewhere deep within me, a growing compassion to help people who can't help themselves. Something passed down from Grandpa to Mom, and now to me.

I attended church with Mom and Dad, but I still didn't connect with God or deal with my anger. The comfortable, familiar atmosphere of my childhood church took the edge off my pain, and to look at me, one would think I was on the mend. In reality, though, I still mouthed the words to hymns and prayers, and felt I nothing. My heart had become so hardened, God's love couldn't penetrate it.

Being closer to Chris also helped me cope. Over the next year, we hung out once in a while, but more often than not, Brian was there too. I started to notice that when Chris walked into a room and sat beside me, Brian left. I wondered if the special bond Chris and I shared made Brian uncomfortable.

That Christmas I attended a party at Chris' childhood home. After our "hello" hug, I handed Chris a gift and went into another room to mingle. Two men sat quite close together on a couch, and I'd just notice one put his hand on the other's leg when Chris came up behind me and said, "Come on, let's get a snack from the kitchen."

The kitchen was occupied as well. Finally, he sat at the dining room table and motioned for me to sit beside him.

"Cathy, I—" He stopped. Tears welled in those familiar eyes. I'd never seen so much frustration in him before.

I tried to joke. "I hope my gift's not that bad."

Chris took a deep breath and his body shuddered.

What could possibly be so serious?

"Let's go outside, Cath." He stood and grabbed a pack of cigarettes.

We stepped outside and he lit up. I must admit, I'd been back almost a year and still found it odd to see him smoke, particularly in light of his childhood lung issues.

"Chris, what's wrong?"

He stared at the ground in silence, taking slow drags on the cigarette and exhaling pensively, as if trying to build up his nerves.

Finally, he said, "Cathy. . . I've gone to gay bars."

Then the tears let loose. He cried nonstop as we stood there awkwardly and I tried to think of something to say.

"It's okay, Chris. Now it's out there. I'm glad you told me."

I didn't ask a lot of questions, or tell him I'd suspected anything. I just let him cry it out.

One might think such an admission would change what we had, and perhaps that's why Chris struggled so long to tell me, but it changed nothing. I loved him every bit as much as I had in the third grade and more. We continued to hang out, only now Brian didn't have to make himself so scarce, though he often did anyway.

We particularly enjoyed the Friday and Saturday night dances at a local restaurant where they pushed tables to the sides of the room and brought in a DJ. I felt safe there, sitting with my circle of friends. They knew me, and I knew them. They asked nothing of me other than friendship. I could handle that. We'd laugh and dance until the place closed, then I'd go home to my predictable life.

Were it not for Ginny, a cantankerous, yet playful paraplegic at the facility where I worked, my routine might never have changed.

Ginny's sense of humor was beyond me. Then again, I couldn't imagine the intense boredom she must have felt pent up all day. She seemed to enjoy a game I called Rag Doll. Despite having almost no motor skills, she could make her body go limp and crumple to the floor when I tried to move her, and then stiffen like a board when I tried to return her to the bed. One late night in July, at about 2 a.m., during yet another of our regular wrestling matches, something gave in my right knee and I went down hard.

I stayed focused long enough to call another employee to come take over the watch, call Chris, and then an ambulance, before going into shock from the pain. A lady in the group home watched over me until the ambulance arrived.

As it turned out, I'd dislocated my knee and had to undergo surgery. My injury forced me to take medical leave while I tried to recover. The doctor's instructions to "take it easy" nearly drove me nuts. I could only take so much inactivity. Finally, one Friday night when rest-induced cabin fever threatened to overwhelm me, I hobbled into the make-shift dance hall in my cast. Chris and Brian were there, as were many other friends. As they all took off for the dance floor, I noticed Bo Schrader watching me from the other side of the room. Bo and his sister were regulars, but we had barely said two words to each other before that night.

He made his way to my table, and I put on my best "not interested" face. Sure, I considered him handsome enough, with his long, coal-black hair and hazel eyes, but I had no plans to start anything. I knew Bo's story. Single dad, recently divorced, two young ones at home. Not for me, thank you.

"Not dancing tonight?" He turned a seat sideways and dropped his tall, slender frame onto it. I pointed to my plaster-covered leg propped on the chair next to me.

"Ah." He nodded, leaning forward so I could hear him over the music. "Well, I don't exactly feel like dancing, so I guess I'll just sit here and keep you company."

Right.

It turned out to be a wonderful evening. I found Bo's kind, sweet manner relaxing, and he had a booming laugh that warmed my heart. I felt no pressure, no underlying motives and I enjoyed talking to him. Over the next few weeks we chatted every weekend while we watched our friends dance.

He told me he'd served in the Marine Corps, and talked about his divorce, which began when his wife had left home unexpectedly, leaving her children behind. For him, the split had been difficult, as it rekindled some of the bitterness he felt when his own parents had divorced during his high school years.

Bo absolutely adored his kids, Ryan, 4, and Brandie, 5, and I loved watching him talk about them. His eyes lit up when he told stories about their antics.

"Maybe I can meet them one day," I'd say, but he'd look away, which I later learned only touched the tip of his protective nature. If the children and I were going to meet, it wouldn't be on a whim.

In early August, still encumbered by my cast, I went on a vacation to Disney World with some friends. Despite all the attractions there, I found myself missing Bo, and wondered whether he was thinking of me. Then one evening, when a meteor shower had been forecast for the entire East Coast, he surprised me with a phone call.

"Hey Cathy, I've got the kids here and we're all outside on a blanket getting ready for the meteors." I could picture his engaging grin right through the phone. "Thought you might want to watch with us."

I laughed and walked out to sit on the deck of our condo, which overlooked Florida's vast coastline. Together, though more than 800 miles apart, we watched the stars dance across the sky.

From the Remnants

Despite Bo's charm, I never expected our relationship to develop past the friend stage. When I started to see signs he wanted more, alarm bells went off in my head. I surprised myself one afternoon by turning to God for advice.

Lord, am I too emotional to do this again? Am I carrying too much baggage? Would that even be fair to him?

My prayers weren't exactly genuine. I still felt way too much anger toward God to believe he would bless me with an answer. After all, I'd prayed for him to save my babies and they'd died, so why should I expect him to listen this time?

Still I did feel peace about dating Bo. Then, when he let me meet his children, I knew he was getting serious.

Bo's tender care for Ryan and Brandie impressed me, and his children were fantastic. The three of them lived in a small house with a wood stove. On cold winter evenings, he would bring the kids home from the sitter after work and put them in bed with their coats on while he lit a fire and fixed dinner. When the house warmed they would join him for dinner around the coffee table.

At first, we kept our dates low-key, mostly watching rental movies at his place while the kids slept in the next room. Sometimes we'd drive down to Big Ditch Lake, where we'd dance to the radio and talk for hours. I felt right being with Bo. He encouraged me, and he listened to me. He never seemed annoyed by my grief. When I watched him with his little ones, showing incredible patience and love, my heart melted. Between that and his soft velvet kisses, I had no choice but to fall in love.

I loved his children, right from the start. As we became more comfortable, we spent more time at each other's homes, until Bo had no problem dropping them at my place when he ran errands. On one such visit, I was heating something in the microwave when the timer buzzed. Brandie jumped up, grabbed little Ryan's hand, and headed for the door.

"Brandie, where are you going?" I leapt ahead of them so they couldn't leave.

"I heard the fire alarm." She nodded gravely at her brother. "It's my job to make sure Ryan gets out safely."

My heart melted. "Oh, sweetie, that wasn't the fire alarm." I knelt down to hug her. "But thank you so much for taking such good care of your little brother."

Another time, the three of them came to my place to pick me up for an outing. When I went out to the car, 4-year-old Ryan leapt out and stood by the car door, ushering me in with a wave and a bow—such an adorable little gentleman.

Daddy sure taught them well.

Late one evening in May, Bo brought me to Big Ditch Lake and walked me to the water's edge. An almost magical mist swirled over the lake, mingling with the reflection of the moon. I thought the night couldn't be lovelier, until he got down on one knee and asked me to marry him. Of course, I said yes.

On a tight budget and with little time to prepare for the wedding, I turned to one of my good friends, David's first wife, Monica, whose mother owned a consignment shop. Monica and my former step-daughter Christina were both in the shop when I arrived to try on wedding dresses. Monica said if I found something I liked, her mother could alter it for me to suit my taste. Nothing really caught my attention, and I had almost given up when Christina pulled me aside.

"What do you think of that one, Cathy?" She pointed to a Cinderella dress tacked high on the wall.

"Oh, my. How could I not have seen that? I think it's gorgeous."

Monica pulled the dress down and I tried it on, falling in love with its wide bell skirt and form-fitting bodice. It fit perfectly, no alterations needed. Problem solved. Then Christina picked out my wedding veil and Monica agreed to be one of my bridesmaids. Her mom made my bridesmaids' outfits, green flowing dresses with rosebud wreaths to wear on their heads.

Chris agreed to serve as an usher. I still remember Mom telling Bo, "You do realize that when you marry Cathy, you get Chris. It's a package deal."

Bo chuckled, and welcomed Chris into the family.

We had a true fairy tale wedding. Bo did everything he could to make the event magical, and it was. I couldn't stop staring at him, standing tall in his white tux with tails, his jet black hair and amazing smile. It was also the hottest day on record in our area, and our rented hall had no air conditioning. However, despite the humidity, our cake with its beautiful fountain remained upright. Our guests changed into shorts after the formal dances and celebrated long into the night. Bo and I then set off on our honeymoon, a tour of amusement parks where we rode as many roller coasters as we could.

Returning to Webster Springs, I embarked on my new life with a positive outlook. As I reflected on all that had changed in so short a time, I was surprised to see God's hand in so many areas of my life. Not only had he led me to a good man, but he brought healing to two broken families by bringing them together. Here was this young girl and boy in need of a mommy, and me in need of a boy and girl. Although I still mourned the loss of my babies, just having Ryan and Brandie in my life patched some of the holes in my heart in a way nothing else could have.

Of course, my new role wasn't without trial. Although I refused to call Ryan and Brandie my stepchildren, it would be months before they called me Mom. The transition was most difficult for now 8-year-old Brandie, who frequently pulled the you're-not-my-mom-so-you-can't-make-me card whenever she wanted to assert her independence.

Great dad that he was, Bo knew his kids and how to deal with them.

"Turn the tables on her," he said, after one particularly bad episode. "You have to make her feel the way she makes you feel. The next time she says you're not her mom, tell her she's not your daughter."

"I can't do that; I'll lose what little bond we have!"

"Trust me." Bo grinned. "She loves you. She's just testing you."

The opportunity to put Bo's advice into action came the next morning, as I was trying to get them into coats and out the door to school. Brandie refused to take the coat I held out for her.

"I'm not wearing that."

"Brandie, you have to; it's freezing out there."

"No I don't. You're not my mother, and you can't make me!"

There it was. The gauntlet had been dropped. My heart felt heavy, but I had to trust Bo knew what he was talking about.

"Fine then. You're not my daughter either, Go!"

Brandie stood still. Her eyes welled up, and her lips quivered. Then she rushed to me, arms open. It took all the strength I could muster not to gather her up.

"Sorry Brandie. If you couldn't hug me before, don't try to hug me now. Off to school you go."

I sent the kids outside and closed the door instead of waiting and waving as I usually did. Then I went into the bedroom, threw myself on the bed, and sobbed like a child.

This better work, Bo.

Six agonizing hours later, Brandie burst through the doors and ran straight into my arms.

"I'm so sorry!

Her swollen eyes told me she'd had a day like mine.

I knelt down to hug her. "I'm sorry too, sweetheart. I know I'm not your mommy, but I'm the only mother in the house right now. And I do love you, but you can't keep talking like that."

"I know. I won't. I promise."

She never did it again.

I continued my studies at Glenville, but dropped to part time as family life began to take greater priority. I graduated in December, 1995, thrilled beyond words to have accomplished my goal despite the many roadblocks. We moved to Elkins, a few miles north of Webster Springs, where I started a crisis intervention job at a long-term facility for people with disabilities.

Just as our family seemed to be settling into a rhythm, I started feeling some familiar symptoms: morning sickness, tiredness . . .

Can it be?

I purchased a home pregnancy kit rather than go to a doctor right away. When I read the results, my heart soared. I ran outside to Bo, who was working in the yard. I waved the confirming stick in the air like a banner.

"We're pregnant, we're pregnant!"

He let out one of his booming laughs and picked me up.

"That's wonderful!" He beamed. "I can't wait to tell the kids."

We started the journey excited and full of joy. At the six-week mark, I started bleeding, and a familiar panic crept into my heart. I raced to the hospital, praying in earnest.

Please, Lord, not again. Please protect my baby.

In reply, God sent Dr. Joseph de Courten, a physician at Davis Memorial Hospital in Elkins.

"Your baby is fine, Cathy." Dr. de Courten gave me a grandfatherly smile as he perused my chart. "But I see you have a history of miscarriages in your family so I am going to put you on limited bed rest for the next few weeks.

During a follow up visit at my 15-week checkup he noted that it was the point at which I'd lost Matthew.

"Because of your family history, I'd like to get you in here for some preventive surgery before you go much further. It's risky, but it could save your child."

I didn't care about the risks. I agreed right away. It was a Wednesday and we scheduled the surgery for the following Monday. The next day someone from the hospital called to tell me they'd had a cancelation for the upcoming Friday and ask if I'd like to move my appointment forward.

Nobody could have known then what a difference those three days would make, but they did. Not only was the operation a success, but Dr. de Courten told me afterward I'd been dilated two centimeters and that if I hadn't come in early, I would have lost my baby over the weekend.

"You're still not out of the woods," he cautioned. "I don't want you to lift a *finger* until this baby is born. Get in bed and stay there, and that's an order."

I quit my job and went home to spend 21 weeks doing absolutely nothing. At first, because we lived in a two-story home, the doctor wouldn't even let me climb stairs. That meant being confined to my bedroom upstairs, leaving the bed only briefly for a bathroom break or my daily five-minute shower.

Bo, Ryan, and Brandie did all they could to help. Bo would pack a cooler of cereal and snacks every morning before he left for work. The kids brought me orange juice and milk in the mornings before school so I could make a breakfast. Then somewhere a door would slam shut, leaving me alone in the quiet nothingness.

In the evenings, Bo brought our dinner upstairs, always going the extra step to make soup or something special that he knew I liked. We ate dinner together, chatting about our hopes for this baby, and praying about her future. I prayed often in the long lonely hours, too, telling God I trusted him, but wondering if I really did.

The stress on Bo during this time must have been incredible. He would work all day, take care of me, care for the kids, do all the laundry, cleaning, and cooking, be available to take the kids to soccer practice, and still manage to carry a 4.0 GPA in his college work. I could hardly believe what an amazing man I'd married.

The bed became my nemesis. After two months of lying in it all day and then trying to sleep there at night, I thought I would go absolutely batty. When I poured out my woes to Dr. de Courten during one of my weekly visits, he eased up a bit on my restrictions, allowing me to spend my days on the couch downstairs. I could take one trip down the steps in the morning to lay on the couch and one trip back upstairs each night. Bo made a bathroom downstairs in a hallway by hanging shower curtains around a portable toilet.

The doctor was wonderful throughout the ordeal. I arrived each week fearful and anxious, but his calm demeanor, gentle words of encouragement and his grandfatherly charm always put me at ease. I left each visit with renewed hopes for my baby's chances.

Moving downstairs helped, but I still had too many hours to think. I worried about this baby constantly, and often slipped back into depression.

One morning, little Ryan ran through the front door disrupting my morning melancholy. He raced over to the couch where I'd wrapped myself around a pillow and he thrust out a fist full of colorful weeds—purple clover, yellow ragweed and thistles.

"Oh, Ryan, thank you." Tears filled my eyes as my heart melted. Ryan smiled broadly as I took the bouquet and then quickly ran back outside.

Perhaps I can make it one more day.

At 36 weeks, I developed preeclampsia. By the time I went in for my Wednesday appointment, my feet had swollen so much that my toes stuck straight up and wouldn't touch the ground, my ankles looked as thick as my thighs, and my eyes had begun to swell shut.

Dr. de Courten took one look at me and sent me directly to the hospital. The nurse there couldn't find a single vein in my swollen arms to insert an intravenous needle. She ended up putting it between my fingers.

Bo arrived almost immediately, having found a long-term sitter for the kids. The staff arranged for him to sleep in my room, and he intended to stay as long as I did. He didn't have to wait past Friday.

"It looks as if your little girl is okay." Dr. de Courten spoke to us calmly, as if he dealt with this sort of thing every day. "But today's the day this young lady will make her debut. I've clipped the stitch we put in place a few months back. In about an hour someone will give you an epidural and we'll get this show on the road."

Within 10 minutes the pain overwhelmed me, and I called the nurse.

"I think I need those meds *now*."

She smiled and walked around the bed toward my feet. "You're probably just feeling anxious. Let's take a look, shall we? I'm sure it's just—oh my!"

The nurse raced off and returned with Dr. de Courten, who ran into the room throwing on his gown. As they took their places around me, I heard the nurse exclaim, "She's getting wild eyed, Doctor, she's getting wild eyed!"

I'd been prepared to go through the birth with the epidural, but the sudden change of plans made that impossible. I think the nurse must have captured that moment of realization.

Bo took my face in his hands and made me focus on him. "You can do this, Cathy." I stared into his eyes and dared to trust.

Thus, little Sierra Alexis Schrader came racing into the world, and she hasn't slowed since.

I didn't know it at the time, but Dr. de Courten had stationed a surgical team outside my room. Afterward, my mom asked him why they'd been there. He took a long breath before he spoke.

"To tell you the truth, I thought I was going to lose the mother. I thought I could at least save the baby."

Mesmerized by this sweet little miracle in our arms, Bo and I thanked Dr. de Courten repeatedly, but he would only wave a hand and point upward.

"Don't thank me, this is God." His eyes misted. "She's God's gift."

I felt a surge of overwhelming love and gratitude for all that God had restored in my life, through Bo, my new marriage, two adorable step-children, and now, this beautiful little girl. Holding my tiny but healthy daughter, I could almost hear him say, "I *am* a good God, Cathy. I *am* here, and I've got you."

Again I found myself pondering the path God had turned me toward that day on the porch. I thought about the path I'd chosen with David, the marriage I'd entered into with no concern for God's will in my life.

Could it be possible God hadn't intended me to marry David? Could it be possible he allows sadness in our lives to bring us back to the right paths?

I won't know the answer to that as long as I'm on this earth, and then it won't even matter, but realizing God still cared so much about me that he would bring me through such trials to this place of miracles restored my faith to a point where I could praise him more earnestly.

God had changed me again, and he had stirred a desire in me to know him more intimately. Little did I know, but over the next few years, God would answer that desire in a most unusual manner.

A NEW PATTERN

"Mom, look at that man and lady waving." Ryan's face pressed against the back window of our pre-owned Ford Taurus. "What are they waving at?"

I had to smile when I recognized Bobby's familiar grin. Nothing made Webster Springs feel more like home than its cast of characters. I noted their dirty clothes and Sissy's odd-fitting, leather-like gray hat, and wondered briefly how they could look so happy when they had so little.

Beside me, Bo winked as we waited at the town's only traffic light.

"Well now, that's our welcome committee." He entered the intersection slowly, waving at Bobby and Sissy. "They're saying 'Welcome to your new home!'"

The kids waved madly at the couple as well, and Bobby and Sissy flashed them gap-tooth smiles. They were both tall and thin. Bobby had a drinking man's gaunt, sunken cheeks, and wore a baseball cap over his dark, greasy hair.

I directed Bo to the home we'd be renting for a while. It was good to be coming back to Webster Springs. With the help of my degree, I had found a job with the county Family Resource Network, and Bo had been hired as an officer in the nearby correctional facility. We hoped our combined salaries would make it possible to start building a house on my parents' property.

My world had been practically restored. Newly married, new step children, newborn baby, new job, and a new outlook on life. From the outside, nobody looking at me could see that lost and broken young woman who had stood on my parents' porch only a few years earlier. On the inside, however, my heart still poked at the open wounds, unable to let them alone long enough to heal.

In some ways, I was afraid to be happy. Despite, or perhaps because of Bo's kind nature, I worried my beautiful life would come crashing down like it did before.

This feels too good to be true.

It made no sense, really. God had given me so much and opened so many doors that I truly wanted to trust him but couldn't quite take the leap. In some areas, I'd made progress. For example, I could now sing praises to God during worship services. However, because he let me down with Tiffany and Matthew, I couldn't bring myself to trust him completely.

I built an emotional brick wall of self-preservation around my heart and allowed few people to see behind it. Even Bo had only temporary access. Any time I felt threatened, I could fling those bricks back up in a second.

I also lost faith in my ability to be assertive without fear of retaliation. Whenever a conversation threatened to make waves, particularly with Bo, my insecurities leapt to the forefront. If he pushed too hard, I'd shut down, leaving him staring hopelessly at my stone face.

"How can you just say nothing, Cathy? This is important and we need to talk about it…don't you even care?"

I'd stare resolutely at the television, or turn to a mindless task like laundry and work in silence, afraid to speak.

Watch it, Cathy, you have a good thing here…don't blow it.

This must have been a difficult time for Bo, who, coming from a history of volatile relationships, also disliked confrontation. To his credit, he showed incredible patience during our exasperating one-sided conversations.

What I couldn't make him understand, perhaps because I didn't understand it myself, was that any type of argument triggered a deep fear I had of losing him. I lived on a tightrope of worry that if I disagreed, he'd find me disagreeable, and that one day he'd just decide I wasn't worth the trouble.

How long before he's had enough? And then what will he do? What if he leaves me, too? Worse, he'd take the kids, and that would crush me.

I kept bricks in hand for "just in case."

One day, I thought, *I might have to stand alone again.*

Sierra's presence seemed too good to be true as well, and my heart remained in a tug-of-war state. I'd be laughing and playing with her one moment, then startled the next by the sobering realization that she was healthy and whole, and real.

Then the questions would start anew.

Why did Sierra survive but not the others?

Why, now that I have all this, won't my pain go away?

Why did you take them God?

Why do I still hurt?

I wondered if perhaps there had been something worse than death waiting for Tiffany and Matthew on the path they'd been heading down. I couldn't imagine what that would be, but I pondered it often, and I continued to question God's decision.

Then there were the reminders. Anniversaries or little incidents and coincidences that would send waves of sadness flooding over me. Easter was particularly tough because Matthew had died at Easter. I'd be fixing Easter baskets for the kids and suddenly realize there should be two more. I'd count up how old my babies would have been by now and just start sobbing.

Or someone would ask me how many children I had. I never quite knew how to answer that, and sometimes would just retreat behind my protective wall.

Fortunately, the good times outweighed the bad during that season. Brandie, now 11, and Ryan, 9, kept us quite busy, as did little Sierra. Brandie and Ryan teased Sierra, as older siblings do, but they also helped care for her, and formed strong bonds. Ryan enjoyed playing with his little sister. Brandie, being 10 years older, engaged less devotedly, but they did come together eventually over a common fondness for horses.

Their age disparity made planning family activities somewhat difficult, but we adapted. Ryan's ball games tended to coincide with Sierra's nap times, for example, so we often had to divide and conquer.

Bo and I set our sights on building a permanent home in Webster Springs. At first, we rented a place in town while we worked out the details, foolishly accepting a verbal renewal agreement. After only six months, the landlord decided to rent our home to someone else and asked us to leave. Neither of us liked the idea of continually moving the kids around, so we bought a trailer and moved that to my parents' property in March 1998. The purchase delayed our house plans, but only temporarily, or so we thought.

At Christmas time, Bo bought me an ornament of a little angel girl lifting a baby angel up to heaven, and we put footprint ornaments on the tree to commemorate the babies' short time on this earth. In the spring, he planted an apple tree in our yard and erected a marker beneath it with their names on it. These gestures helped immensely.

Bo somehow understood that I couldn't just pretend nothing had happened, and he gave me space to grieve when I had to. I believe much of Bo's compassion came from experiencing his own past hurts and losses.

Essentially, we were both wrestling with a weak, but yearning faith. We both came from spiritually strong families, and we didn't know at the time, but our parents had been praying for us. Deep down, we both knew that the only true way to heal would be to push forward, keep reading the Bible, and attend regular church services, and so we started looking for a church.

We chose the Emmanuel Assembly of God because of its proximity, and because they had a fantastic youth program. The pastor, Pastor Marty, and his wife Alida were strong teachers and taught us both a lot about faith, believing the Bible, and standing on the Word of God.

As I became more comfortable, I joined the church's Praise Team. I felt closer to God when I sang than at any other time, as if my spirit were reaching out to him. Still, I stopped short of putting down the bricks and relinquish my life to God's control. Something simple like noticing Tiffany's approaching birthday had the power to shut me down. I'd slip back to "square one," mouthing the words in church and piling up the bricks as my defense mechanism—walling off my emotions made it easier to feel nothing. How grateful I am that Bo stood with me during those times.

Being closer to Chris also helped. He had graduated and taken a job as a physical therapist in Webster Springs, so we saw each other more often. No matter how long between chats, we could always pick right up as if we'd been apart only minutes instead of days and weeks. After our initial awkward conversation about his lifestyle, I hadn't brought it up much, except once, when I asked him why he'd taken so long to tell me, and why he'd cried so much that night he *did* tell me.

"I don't know," he said quietly. "I guess I was embarrassed."

Chris and I did have an interesting conversation a few years down the road. I don't know how it started, but we'd been sharing a long silence over lunch one day when he looked up at me and asked, "Cathy, have you ever been going down a path that you didn't know how to get off?"

I wasn't sure I knew what he meant, but I didn't push.

"Once or twice. I guess we all have moments like that. I usually turn to God when that happens."

He fell back into silence for a while. I knew he was contemplating his Methodist upbringing, which he'd walked away from years earlier. He didn't doubt God's existence, but perhaps his love.

"I do pray, Cath, but it's like I'm praying to the ceiling."

"You think he doesn't hear you?" I touched his arm. "He does. Chris, God wants you, just as you are. You don't have to fear changing for him. If he wants you to change, he will change you."

I saw a brief flicker of hope in his eyes, but sadness swallowed it up.

"Well, you and I have different beliefs." He pulled a cigarette from his pack and rose from the table to light it outside. We didn't address it again.

My new job with the Family Resource Network gave me purpose and a sense that my work mattered. Essentially, I helped link resources to people who needed them among Webster County's impoverished and needy population.

One of my early victories in that job was the Back to School Bash, which began in 1998, just after I arrived. At issue were 65 local school students whose families could not afford to clothe them sufficiently. I met with area merchants, many of whom made donations or gave me certificates for shoes and clothing to hand out.

I remember a small, quiet girl with long blond hair and serious blue eyes. When I gave her a certificate for free shoes, she didn't quite understand, but she accepted it solemnly. A few weeks later, I saw her on the street. Or rather, she saw me, and she came running, braids flying behind her.

"You're the lady who gave me my new shoes!" She started dancing around me, showing off the shoes as she twirled and just glowing with joy. "Thank you, thank you! I love them so much!"

If someone had handed me a million dollars right then, it wouldn't have meant more than watching that little girl dance. Seeing her joy and gratitude made me want to do even more. Over the next few years we expanded the program to other communities, and it continues today, helping hundreds of children every year.

In addition to finding clothing, I ran coat drives, food drives, coordinated Christmas Angel Tree sponsorships, established a training area in the municipal building for continuing education, and helped train small community groups in leadership and community development. I also served on the Community Collaborative Board, which involved attending many meetings and national conferences, where I networked and learned ways we could help even more. Wherever we identified needs, we looked for resources to fill them.

In 1999, I added "Litter Control Chair" to my list of responsibilities, which presented a fascinating, rewarding challenge. I'd always enjoyed conservation work. As a child I'd joined the Youth Conservation program, which sponsored many local clean-up projects. This new position helped me build on that foundation, as I promoted state initiatives like Adopt-a-Highway, the Youth Environmental Program, and Tire Amnesty collections.

One of my favorite aspects of this type of work was meeting with volunteers and organizations from throughout the county. I met many enthusiastic, community-minded people, and became adept at encouraging people to pitch in or support local projects. Often I integrated their varied skills and passions into projects that met common goals. For instance, to solicit help in clearing up a nearby open dump, we showed the Development Authority how the results would improve tourism, and brought the Health Department and parents on board because it would reduce the breeding ground for mosquitoes and reduce the risk of encephalitis. Then we involved the Scouts and school children with a poster contest to raise awareness and used their posters as publicity. The bank donated savings bonds for the winners, as well as to the student in Tire Amnesty who encouraged the greatest amount of tire recycling. With just one project, we brought the entire community together through hard work and a common goal, with beautiful results.

I also found I had a knack for seeing how one man's trash could be someone else's treasure. As part of the FRN, I sought ways to reuse and re-purpose items. When a local potter needed a specific type of plastic as part of his pottery-making process, I found some at an area restaurant—plastic holders for take-out containers that would have otherwise been thrown away. These types of recycling and beautification projects earned Webster Springs eight first-place, three second-place and one third-place "WV Make It Shine Clean County" awards during the 13 years I served as Litter Control Chair. My department moved tons of resources through that small office over the years.

I'd like to think I also set a good example for the youth who participated in the events. When she was older, Sierra's Girl Scout troop recycled plastic grocery bags one year. Their work not only made them feel like contributors in the attempt to make a cleaner earth, but also earned them a trophy and a cash prize through the Division of Environmental Protection's Youth Environmental Program.

Of course, the job wasn't always easy, and it wasn't without the occasional calamity. During the planning stage for a small-town clean-up project, I told the local mayor the County would pick up items left on the edge of Main Street. I thought she understood I'd been referring to tires and other large items people might come across *during the cleanup*, but the message to the community implied we'd pick up ALL trash on the road's edge. People came in droves, some from nearby counties, toting everything they had. They piled up a wall of trash approximately 10 feet high and several feet deep that ran from one end of town to the other. We had to ask local authorities to rope off Main Street, and we worked with the Division of Highways and a local equipment contractor to bring in dump trucks and end loaders to haul off the debris. Someone calculated we collected about 9,000 tons of steel, 3,000 tires and 85 tons of other trash. On the up-side, the town certainly looked clean, and it was a good lesson on effective communication. I returned to my office to find my "friends" had hung toy tires all over my door.

Between 2002 and 2003, I also helped establish 17 emergency shelters in Webster County. Most were set up in churches, and volunteers received training to manage the shelters in an emergency. An ice storm hit in February, 2003 knocking out power across the county and making travel impossible. People flocked to the local churches for shelter and emergency supplies. I'm sure those shelters saved lives.

In 2003, I also received the Regional Crystal Starfish Award for "Continual Demonstration of Family Centered Practice." The award represented the now-familiar story of a child throwing beached starfish back into water who was told there were too many starfish for her efforts to make a difference and that she was wasting her time. The child said, "I made a difference to that one." In a nutshell, that's how I felt about my work. We may not have changed the world, but if what we did changed the world for a few people, our efforts were worthwhile.

I didn't know it at the time, but in working on these projects, my skill set expanded. God was honing my organizational expertise, teaching me to trust myself and others, and, under Pastor Marty's teaching, deepening my faith in the Lord.

Pastor Marty had an extraordinary gift for healing prayer. We saw many people healed in that church, and it gave us confidence in prayer. But his wife impressed me the most in this area. She had been diagnosed with stage-4 breast cancer, and had received prayer. When members of the congregation offered to pray for her as well, she politely refused and walked away.

One Sunday she spoke before the congregation. "From this moment on, I ask that you not pray for my healing. Marty has prayed for me, and I am healed. I will see out my remaining nine months of chemo, because I believe that is God's intended process for me.

However, from today forward, when you pray for me, offer only praise and thanksgiving to God for my healing."

Beside me, Bo's wheels were turning. I knew she'd impressed him with her faith. Nine months later, when doctors operated to remove her tumor, they discovered she was cancer-free, just as God had promised her.

At home, I gained confidence in my roles as wife and mother. Other parents may have considered me a bit overprotective of Sierra, but I wanted her to grow up untethered by the world's expectations for her. I fought hardest when it came to well-meaning advice that might squash her independent spirit. Sierra started dreaming big dreams at age 4, explaining to anyone who'd listen that she wanted a horse. I ignored the nay-sayers who called it a stupid idea.

"Tell you what, Sierra," I said. "If you're serious and save your money, one day you might see that dream come true." I had no idea she'd actually do it, but that's for another chapter.

I started believing perhaps my life was going to be fine—that my self-preservation tactics and hard work would enable me to succeed. However, I had no idea what was coming, or that the Lord had prepared me for battle by teaching me about myself and my faith so I could stand firm in the face of the trials headed my way. A series of events occurred over the next months that should have scared me out of my wits, but instead, I found myself gaining strength and wondering how it would all come together…

FIERY FURNACE

"Oh, Mom, I love it!"

Sierra solemnly accepted the backpack, tracing the horse with her 6-year-old fingers. I'd been fortunate to find the satchel at the consignment shop. It seemed hardly used at all.

Bo, stretched out on his easy chair, nodded his approval over the top of his newspaper. Brandie, 16, had left with friends, and Ryan was in the back yard, soaking up the last hours of summer.

As I watched my sweet girl fill her new bag with notebooks and crayons, my heart lurched. Suddenly, all the back-to-school thrill became smothered in darkness.

I never got to watch Tiffany do this. She would have been starting middle school this year.

I rose and quickly raced to my bedroom, where I fell onto the bed, sobbing.

"Cathy? What just happened back there?" Bo followed me into the room and settled his lean body along-side mine. He brushed back my hair and searched my red face for answers.

"I don't know!" I sobbed. "It's all this back-to-school, I guess. I can't stop wondering. . . Oh Bo, my babies. I miss them so much."

He held me a while then went back to help Sierra pack. We both knew I'd be all right soon. I just had to cry it out.

On August 30 of that year, 2003, while dressing for work, I suddenly envisioned a day in my future in which I knew all was well. I cannot describe it here, as I'm still not comfortable sharing it, but I will say it left me with such a strong, lingering sense of God's power that I hit my knees in prayer and I fasted for days in an attempt to learn more. Even then, I didn't tell anyone about it, but I prayed and continued to read the Bible, searching for answers.

Then I came across a verse in Jeremiah that captured my heart. It said, *"For I know the plans I have for you," declares the Lord, plans to prosper you and not to harm you, plans to give you hope and a future."*

It made so much sense. God was establishing a plan for my life. I continued to fast, wanting desperately to see more of the picture. Four days later, while driving home from work, I had to stop at a construction site to wait for the oncoming line of cars to pass through the zone. As I sat at the front of my line, facing the "stop sign man," a peaceful feeling washed over me and I heard what I know now was the Holy Spirit.

"The path is laid out for you. It's done. You just have to walk in it."

I started laughing and couldn't stop, as this spiritual joy I couldn't explain just bubbled up inside me. The sign man looked bewildered, because I sat alone. I laughed all the way home. I had no idea what the message meant, but I believed it was linked to my vision from a few days earlier.

The following week, Bo called me at work.

"Cathy, are you praying about something?"

"Sort of." I still hadn't told him.

"Well, I'm here in the kitchen standing over the trash can, peeling potatoes." He paused. "So, the Holy Spirit just stood me up and said, 'It is done.' I have no idea what you're praying about but it's done."

"Okay." I had no idea what else to say.

The next week, although I felt quite sure the Holy Spirit nudged me to step out and sing at our church homecoming, I didn't do it. Instead, I allowed fear to stop me. I berated myself later for not obeying.

Mom called soon afterward.

"Cathy, I have no idea what's going on, but the Holy Spirit told me to call you. Do you know the story in the Bible about Jesus feeding the 5,000?

"Yes."

"Remember he took the bread and fish to feed the people?"

"Yes." *Where is this going?*

"Well, it doesn't say this in the Bible, but remember that when the disciples stepped out with the baskets, Jesus didn't make a big mound of food. They went out with empty baskets and He filled them as they went. Now, I have no idea what you're going through but you just step out and he will fill the baskets."

I could only weep.

Next time, I'll step out, I vowed.

Something big must be waiting ahead.

These little lessons landed regularly on my heart, or at least on the wall around it. God wanted me to learn from them. Somehow I knew a big test was coming and that my success or failure would be determined according to my level of obedience, as well as my faith and trust in God. I took comfort, however, in knowing that God had already seen the plan through to the end, as he'd told me repeatedly, "It is done."

Over the next few weeks I often felt overwhelmed and too small for whatever waited ahead. One day in October, while listening to a Christian music cassette tape as I delivered the FRN monthly newsletter, God put my anxiety to rest. Every time I stopped the car, the tape started back at the beginning. I even tested it to see if I was crazy, but I was not. It kept restarting. The strangeness of this made me wonder if God was trying to get my attention.

I have to find somewhere to pray.

Without a moment's hesitation, I left my route and headed home. Back in my bedroom, I kneeled to pray.

Jesus I need to know you're with me. I need to feel your presence.

I sensed Jesus kneeling in front of me and something made me reach out my hands. I felt my hands cup around his face, his warmth emanating through me. I then felt his hands cover mine and I heard what I can only describe as a voice in my spirit saying, "We can do this."

Emotionally undone, I started to cry as I repeated, "We can do this, we can do this." I then wrote down the scripture Philippians 4:13—*I can do all things through Christ who strengthens me*, which I posted on my mirror and recited often.

Needless to say, as I became more in tuned with God, I knew He wanted me to do *something*, but not what. He showed me the future, and the peace I'd find at the end, but he told me nothing about the road I would travel to reach it.

I passed my national exam to become a Professional Community and Economic Developer. To me, it represented another plaque on the wall; to God, I suspect it meant I was one step closer to being ready for the trial heading my way.

The trial began that November like a rippling wave, when Bo, who never got sick, went to bed early complaining of a toothache. Then he woke me in the middle of the night.

"Cathy, you have to get me to the hospital now!"

I woke Ryan, who helped me get Bo into the car, and I raced to the hospital. As soon as we arrived, he started going into convulsions and having seizures. Between that and his spiking fever, the doctor quickly diagnosed a serious infection, but couldn't determine the source.

"We're sending him to Charleston." The doctor's face told me that every moment the situation worsened.

Because all available ambulances had left on runs, the hospital staff arranged for Bo to fly to Charleston via helicopter, where he spent nearly a week receiving antibiotics. His seizures terrified me, rattling his teeth with such violence I thought they would shatter. Still, the doctors couldn't find the cause.

Then came even more terrifying news. One of the doctors actually decided to send him home. Apparently, the hospital needed more beds.

"What do you mean, send him home? What if he has a seizure?"

"Well Ma'am, just stay with him and make sure he doesn't hurt himself." The doctor barely looked at me.

Bo complained that his tooth still hurt, so I offered to take him to the dentist the next day. The dentist solved the mystery.

"He has an abscessed tooth, and the infection has spread into his bloodstream."

I could only stare. "Will he be all right?"

"Yes." The dentist smiled. "The doctors actually saved him by giving him antibiotics."

Bo told me later that his grandmother had died from an infected tooth. I had much to be thankful for that night when I prayed.

I sometimes wonder whether God had been thinking at that moment, "You haven't seen anything yet," because, even as I prayed, that tidal wave of trial forming off shore had started heading toward us.

✗ ✗ ✗ ✗ ✗ ✗

Bo grimaced as he stood up from the couch.

"Babe, are you okay?" My former U.S. Marine generally had a high tolerance for pain, but I could sense he'd hit his limit.

"I don't think so, Cathy. It seems worse than ever."

Bo's back had suffered a serious blow in a car accident many years earlier that led to degenerative disc disease. Essentially, the padding between his vertebrae had eroded, causing great pain.

Over the next few weeks, as the pain worsened, Bo took increasingly more medication just to be able to function. Finally, the pain became too much.

"I can't deal with it anymore, Cathy." Bo's eyes widened in disbelief.

Bo's supervisors approached him at work, concerned that he could not safely care for himself or the inmates in his condition. So, after six years of service, he left the correctional facility.

I couldn't argue. They'd made the right decision. Still, a knot of fear formed in my gut. *How can we make it on half our income?*

The tidal wave had crested, and I knew it was going to engulf us. Determined not to panic, I grabbed my Bible.

I've got to stand on scripture. I've got to find something to stand on.

Trying to ignore the fear, I searched frantically through the pages. Finally, I landed on Job 23:10, and I knew it was for me.

"For He knows the path that I take when he has tried me, and I shall come forth as gold."

I stared at those words, feeling fear and comfort at the same time. Reminded that fire purifies gold, I realized God was about to use fire to remove impurities from our lives and prepare us for what he had planned next.

At first I nearly fled, as if I had somewhere to flee *to*. But I remembered how my attempts to battle trial on my own when the babies died had nearly destroyed me. I wasn't sure I could survive something like that again. Then I thought of all the small lessons God had led me through in the previous months and knew he'd given me what I needed to make it through this time. I had a better understanding of what God *can* do, and we belonged to a church family we knew we could lean on.

Besides, he had shown me my future, and I knew everything would be all right. I braced myself and remembered the warmth of his face in my hands.

"We can do this, God."

That Sunday, I stood before our congregation and spoke briefly about what was happening in our lives. I told them the trial ahead was going to be difficult, and asked that they pray for our family, but I also assured them that we'd be okay.

"Bo and I are headed into the furnace, like Shadrach, Meshach, and Abednego." I could just envision us walking into that dark, fiery cavern, and the hot iron door slamming behind us. "I don't know how long we're going to be there, or what we're going to have to endure. I only know it's going to be a trial, but God has promised that we're going to come forth as gold."

The tidal wave hit full force with the April bills. I wrestled with contrasting beliefs: One, that God would take care of us, and the other, that it was up to me to get us all through this.

Bo's pain continued to worsen. His back hurt so much, he often had to take pain medicine just to prepare to roll over in the bed. I'd watch helplessly as he clutched the headboard and pull himself over slowly, using every ounce of strength he could muster.

On the rare good days, he attended Sunday service, but he usually stayed home. Not only would he have suffered through the uncomfortable trip to the church, once there he'd barely be able to sit still through the service.

A typically quiet person anyway, Bo rarely talked about the pain, but the heaviness of his frustration filled the home. Our recently purchased kayak mocked him from the back yard. He'd been such an active man, biking, camping, and playing ball with Ryan, that sitting on the sidelines must have been excruciating.

He spent the days lying on his recliner in silence, feet up, television on, nearly lethargic from the strong pain meds he had to take. I'd bring him dinner in his chair and watch while he winced his way upright to accept it. He hadn't laughed in ages. I worried he might become depressed, and I do believe there were times he gave in to the temptation.

Once in a while I'd look at my sweet Bo and think, "This is not the man I married," but I loved him so much, and he'd always been there for me, so it never occurred to me to do anything but take up his side of the partnership as long as he needed me to.

I found a second job waiting tables at a diner in town, which helped, but didn't come close to making up for Bo's salary.

Working at a diner. Who would have thought?

Mom's words echoed in my head, "Get a diploma so you can work where you *want* to, not where you *have* to." So much for that. There simply wasn't any other option. I already worked full time during the day, so I needed an evening job, and in a small rural town, you take what you can get.

It's okay. I can do this. I'm in control.

But as events unfolded, I realized I wasn't at all in control. Looking back, I can see God had been changing me through this time, pruning some rather unhealthy traits from my character, all the while, still meeting my family's every need.

He began with my ego, showing me that, while I hadn't been aware of it, deep in my heart I found working in a diner a bit beneath my status. Despite my misery, I tried to maintain an upbeat personality, particularly with the customers, but I struggled occasionally to shine over the shame that had crept into my heart. I felt as if I were leading a double life, attending board meetings during the day to discuss complex plans for the future of Webster County, and then serving dinner to those same attendees later that evening. I can still recall the mayor doing a double-take one night as I set his coffee in front of him.

"I didn't know you worked here, Cathy." He seemed to shift uncomfortably in his seat. I'd met with him and the others at his table only three hours earlier in the FRN conference room in the county hospital.

"Surprise." I gave him a tight-lipped smile. "Just for a little while. We're, um…thinking of building a house."

Well, it's true. Sort of.

Oddly, were I to really scrutinize the customers, they probably weren't the slightest bit concerned about my working there. I projected my shame onto them, and it bounced back as a perceived judgment.

Besides, as I spent time with my co-workers at the diner, I realized they held no better, and no worse, status than I. They worked hard and clearly cared for one another and their customers. I enjoyed getting to know them. In particular, I had many conversations with the cook, Ruby, and with her daughter, Lynn, who waited tables with me.

Ruby, a thin, outspoken woman, had what seemed like a cloud of sadness hanging over her. We got along well enough, but she didn't let me past her wall and I didn't let her past mine.

My dual personality took on a third dimension when I came home each night after most everyone had fallen asleep and shifted into "Mom mode." Although Brandie then 17, and Ryan, 15, were relatively self-sufficient, 7-year-old Sierra needed more than just a sometimes mother. I struggled to establish a "normal" home life for each of them. Every night I packed lunches, washed laundry, cleaned the house, and whenever I could, I arranged my schedule around ball games and school events, which meant usually working the closing shift. When I couldn't be home, I'd call in the evenings to make sure everyone had settled down for the night.

The second area God tested during this time involved my trust. Despite all I saw him accomplish, I still found myself struggling to resolve difficult situations alone, and always to no avail. Our finances remained in a dismal state, but never crossed a certain line.

Then I happened across God's assurances in Matthew 6:25-34, which I keep in my heart even today. It's too long for this story, but I've included it at the end of the book. Essentially, God tells us that we needn't worry about anything. He's not only aware of all we need, he also has a plan to provide it.

As I looked back on our ordeal, God's promise rang true the entire time. We never went without something we needed. We had enough to get by and not a bit more, and every time money ran out, God stepped in. There were times I couldn't afford a box of laundry detergent and I'd come home to find someone had left a bag of groceries on our steps containing, not only detergent, but also toilet paper and everything else I needed to make it until pay day.

One Sunday morning, I was feeling particularly anxious because Bo's pain medication had run out, but we didn't have the $49.60 to refill his prescription.

"We're just going to go to church and let God worry about it," I told him. We dressed and headed out, and after I'd settled Bo in the pew and we prayed together for a few minutes, I rose to take my place in the choir. That's when Nancy walked up and hugged me.

"You've been on my heart, Cathy." She slipped something into my hand. "I just wanted to bless you."

As she walked away, I looked into my hand and nearly fell over. I returned to Bo with tears in my eyes, handing him the $50 bill. "For your meds," I choked out.

I knew people were aware of our story, at least a portion of it, particularly since I'd announced the coming tidal wave to our congregation. It helped to know they prayed for us. Sometimes, as I learned months later, God prompted them to do more.

When we received a three-day notice that the power company would be cutting us off because of payments owed and late fines. I couldn't bring myself to tell anyone. I prayed that God would help us, and recalled all the previous times he'd come through.

"We need you, Lord. I don't know what we're going to do."

The next day, again as I sat in the church, the pastor's wife Alida settled into the pew beside me and put her hand on my shoulder. "Cathy, you know we pray for you and your family all the time. Well, this week while we were praying we realized sometimes you have to do more than pray." She handed me an envelope. "Use this wherever you need to. And have a great day."

From the Remnants

If ever I had to "lean not on my understanding," it was when I opened that envelope, for the amount covered the entire bill from the power company, to include the fines. Just enough, and not a penny more.

On some days, my personal and professional roles would overlap, and I'd get a glimpse of how everyone's lives intertwine. For instance, one day, a pastor named Steve from a nearby church called Compassionate Hope Church of God, stopped by my office. He said his church wanted to take on a project and asked what the community needed.

With Brandie's High School prom on the horizon, I'd been frustrated that I couldn't afford to buy her a dress. Even the dresses at the consignment shop were way out of our budget. When you're struggling, a sign that said, "Only $50" isn't so special.

"The girls around here could use prom dresses." The words just blurted out. "They can't afford the two or three hundred dollars it takes to get dresses for one of the most important days of their high school lives."

Pastor Steve's eyes lit up and he took the idea back to his congregation. Almost immediately, his church took up dress donations and started The Fairy Tale Closet, which is still going on today. They helped 30 or 40 girls that first year, and now have such a surplus that it's open to surrounding counties. They also set up a hair and nail service for the girls every year.

During one of the last years I helped with this project, a young lady who was getting married called to ask if she could get a dress there. Of course, I said yes, and even suggested she bring her bridesmaids.

When the bride-to-be arrived, we found a darling white dress for her, but couldn't find matching dresses for the bridesmaids. We did however, find the same dress in four different colors, so she had a rainbow wedding. How amazing is this God, who provided for me, for Brandie, and for countless other young girls over the years just through my situation?

A third area of my life where God certainly had set his pruning shears addressed my humility, or lack of it. Although I spent nearly every day addressing the needs of the many in our community, I'd not humbled myself to serve on a personal level. Had I pondered this, I might have reasoned that I had nothing to give. I could barely pay my own bills, so how could God expect me to help others?

But he did, and he told me so, in a direct and frequent manner.

It began at what I called The Intersection, one afternoon as I sat alone in my car, waiting for the light to change. Bobby and Sissy were not at their usual post, and I briefly wondered what might have happened to them.

"Bring them home."

The voice sounded so clearly in my ear, I looked to the passenger seat to make sure nobody had crept in. Empty, of course.

"What? Do you mean now?" I don't want them in my house.

"Bring them home."

For some reason, I knew this wasn't a literal command, just as I knew this was the Holy Spirit's prompting. An image flashed before me of Sissy, clean and walking down the street surrounded by people. I pictured her laughing, not with the bashful smiles she offered strangers on the street corner, but with the joyful laugh of a truly happy woman.

"So if you're not saying to bring them to my house, what am I supposed to do, exactly?"

I'm not proud to say that when I didn't receive a response, I did nothing, trying to shake it off as my overactive imagination. The next day, as I approached the corner I noticed they were missing again. It occurred to me they might need food or other supplies. I tried to ignore the impulse, but it wouldn't leave me alone.

"Fine, I'll go to the store."

Frustration nearly overwhelmed me as I stood in the grocery aisles. I had only a small amount of money, which I'd intended to spend on our own food.

"I don't even know what they want, Lord! You're going to have to show me."

I purchased what I thought were basic necessities and headed toward the shack on the lane. Recalling the lack of parking at the bottom of the hill, I parked by a restaurant on an upper street and walked down, carrying my box of goods.

Please don't let anyone see me. Please, please, please.

"Do you need a ride, Cathy?"

I forced a smile over my reddening cheeks as I shook my head. "No thanks, Barb, I'm fine."

Nothing to see here...move on please...don't watch where I'm going.

And again. And again. Five times in all, people stopped to offer help. The entire town knew where I was. At least, it felt that way.

After what seemed an eternity, I arrived at Bobby's place, still grumbling at God.

"I don't even know what you want me to say to these people. You're going to have to help me with that, too, Lord."

The old shack they'd lived in when I was younger had been replaced by a beat-up trailer, perhaps something donated by the county. When Sissy answered the door, her face lit up.

"I just wanted to drop this off." I shoved the box forward. "I haven't seen you in a couple of days and I missed you out at the light waving at us. I thought I'd stop by to check on you.

"Yeah, he hurt his back." She looked back inside. I noticed the walls behind her seemed to have been painted black. "I don't know when we'll be back."

Sissy took the box and thanked me. I'd probably spent all of ten dollars, but by her smile, you would have thought it was Christmas.

I turned to leave and hiked back to my car. Then, as many Christians might do in that situation, I put the moment behind me.

Check, check, done.

Nope. God had more plans for me regarding Bobby and Sissy.

They soon returned to their post at The Intersection, but they were even more prominent at the intersection in my spirit. Throughout the year I'd frequently think of them for no reason, and feel an impulse to act. At first I tried to respond with exasperation, but eventually I learned to obey the impulses, because ignoring them never made them go away.

Late in February, I felt a strong urge to get Sissy something special. I rummaged through my pockets and came up with a small bit of change, not even a dollar, which I took into the local convenience store. There, on the clearance shelf, I spotted a leftover Valentine's Day chocolate shaped in a heart, just within my budget.

I shrugged, turned over my change to the clerk, and walked across the street with my purchase. Sissy beamed as if I'd given her a diamond ring.

"Oh, thank you." Her eyes sparkled. "It's my birthday!"

My heart jumped. Glancing upward I sighed.

You could have told me.

Over time I understood that my own situation paled in comparison to others, and there would always be someone I could help, sometimes by giving, and at other times by setting the example.

One day I passed a flower shop and thought of Sissy. I felt prompted by the Holy Spirit to get her a bouquet.

Yes, Lord. I think she would like that.

I entered the shop, where the florist was a friend I knew through a community development project.

"Hi Cathy!" She smiled brightly. "What can I do for you today?"

"I'd like to send some flowers."

"Sure! To whom?"

"Sissy, (everyone knew them and where they lived.)

In that instant, her entire demeanor changed, and she looked at the floor.

"I'm sorry, we're really busy today. Unfortunately, we're not able to make deliveries."

I didn't push. I'd been in her shoes just a few months earlier. "That's okay. You put them together and I'll deliver them."

Her shoulders lifted and she nodded before heading to the back of the shop. When she returned, I accepted the bouquet and said quietly, "You know, we pass people on the street every day who just need a smile. If we would just stop and let them know we care, imagine the impact we could make on people's lives."

She actually started tearing up. "That's the most beautiful thing I've heard in a long time. Here, I'll give you a discount."

I delivered the bouquet to the trailer, this time walking down the hill with my head held high. Bobby answered the door this time, raising one eyebrow as I thrust the flowers forward.

"Did you know she was sick?"

"She is? No, I didn't."

Why are you surprised, Cathy?

From the Remnants

"Well, this is very kind of you. Thank you."

"Don't thank me, God wants her to have them." I turned around, but not before I saw the other eyebrow rise.

I wasn't sure where those words had come from, but I liked them. I started writing short Bible verses or "Jesus Loves You" on gifts when I brought them. I didn't even know if they could read or write, but that didn't stop me. As I became more familiar with the couple, I learned that Sissy's leather-like hat was merely a dilapidated hat brim worn like a crown around her gray hair—the top had come off. I also learned that the walls in their trailer were not black, but soot-covered from their wood stove, because the trailer lacked proper ventilation and plumbing.

Back at home, I felt as if I were losing ground. My sweet Bo had retreated into a shell of depression. He still attended church services when he could, but those times became more and more rare. Most days he could barely move, and it hurt me to watch this former Marine and active outdoorsman relegated to the recliner, unable to even mow the lawn.

My taking a second job exacerbated his depression. He had completed the paperwork to qualify for disability assistance, and that money helped a little, but he saw it as *his* duty to care for the family and hated that I had to work so hard. In those rare occasions when we'd talk about his situation, he'd become defensive and take offense at my words. I could only pray and try to get him to church on Sundays so he could hear God's voice.

Not that I was always the strong one. One afternoon, after months of living on the receiving end of our community's generosity, something in me snapped. I simply couldn't muster the emotional energy to make one more trip to the food pantry or accept yet another discretely passed envelope of cash. It wasn't a matter of pride, but sheer weariness from so much needing.

How long, Lord, must we stay in this furnace?

The counselor assigned to Bo as part of his disability application process turned out to be a friend of ours, a sweet, compassionate woman named Loren. We shared our frustration regarding mounting bills, which had reached the $1,200 mark, with more coming due soon, and Loren opened her check book.

"I have a jewelry ministry." She started filling in a check. "I make and sell jewelry and use the proceeds to help people in need. I'd like to give you $800."

Bo's hopeful smile disappeared when he looked at me.

"If you want it, you take it." I looked down at my hands. "I'm not taking another thing."

My weariness had taken its toll, and with nobody else to blame, I directed my internal anger at Bo.

If only he would step up and start taking care of the family...

The shame I felt for thinking this kept me quiet. I knew if there were any way he could have worked, he would have, in an instant.

Bo wisely accepted the money, giving Loren a grateful grin. Then he turned and handed the money to me. It was just enough to provide us some breathing room, and turned out to be one of the last times we needed assistance.

Besides emotional energy, my physical endurance had waned by that time as well. I ran constantly, from one job to another, switching clothes and mind-set enroute. At the diner I rarely sat down because a waitress's place is everywhere, so my energy drained away long before my shift ended. Still I had to drag myself home to tackle the mountain of chores and tasks that must be addressed before the next day. It brought new meaning to the term, "collapsing into bed."

Of course, on paper, that makes me sound like a super hero. In reality, although I managed, I didn't thrive. I spread myself so thinly that nothing received sufficient attention. Not only that, but I cried often. In fact, I remember the exact moment I gave up.

It was a Wednesday night. I'd taken some time off from the diner to attend an evening service at Emmanuel. I'd felt so tired all night, the words from the service hadn't been able to penetrate my brain. I walked toward the restaurant with lead in my feet, thinking about follow-up tasks for a meeting I'd attended that day at the office, the hours ahead of me at the diner, chores waiting at home, bills coming due. In my mind I pictured myself carrying sacks on my back. I saw the sacks become heavier, their weight sending me to my knees, but still I refused to relinquish the burden.

I stopped in my tracks.

That's it, God. I can't walk another step. I'm done. I'm quitting the diner job. I'm tired, I hurt, and this is getting me nowhere.

I'd failed, which was a humbling enough realization for an overachiever. But here I stood, confessing my shortcomings to God, as if he didn't know already. I pleaded with him to understand.

Lord, I can't do what you've asked me to do. All this weight on my shoulders, it's too much. You want it? Take it! I just can't carry it another minute!

I could feel the anger surging inside me and I lashed out again.

God, if you're going to step in, you need to do it now!

I didn't hear so much as feel the quiet, loving voice, as if he'd spoken to my spirit.

"Cathy, you're just where I need you to be right now."

Shame washed over me. I could hardly believe I'd spoken to him that way, and yet, he'd responded only with kindness. A picture flashed through my mind of Ruby and Lynn at the diner and immediately I understood that this time it wasn't about me, but about them. For some reason, God had put me in their lives, not the other way around.

I lowered my head and offered up my meekest apology. "God, I don't know what you're up to, but I'll try to trust you. If you want me to go back, I'll go back."

And I did, but this time with purpose. I tried to examine everything with God's plan in mind. I smiled more at the customers, and I talked more with my coworkers.

If something is supposed to come of this, Lord, show me where I'm to look.

I didn't have to wait long.

On a particularly slow evening, I started talking to Ruby about God. She seemed tough on the outside, but I'd learned differently over the time we spent together. Her gray hair pulled back in a tight bun, and her raspy voice attested to the difficult road she'd travelled. Ruby knew I shared her tiredness, but I made sure she also knew I felt joy at times, particularly when I sang in the choir.

"Do you attend church, Ruby?"

"Yeah, I used to." She looked over my head to the past. "I plan to go back one day. If my husband would go . . ."

Then she seemed to remember I was there.

"I just haven't gotten around to it." She ducked back into the kitchen and the conversation ended. But after that I brought God into the conversation whenever I saw an opportunity, not in a nagging way, but little morsels here and there. I praised him when we had a particularly beautiful day, and I told them about the times God answered our prayers at home.

One rainy day around this time, I ran into Bobby and Sissy in the convenience store. We chatted briefly, but I had to rush the conversation along to make a scheduled meeting at the office. The rain about drenched me as I ran to my car. I sat at the store exit, watching Bobby and Sissy come out, carrying their meager bags of groceries, and start down the road toward their trailer. I paused before pulling onto the street. I had prepared to turn right toward my office but they were walking to my left.

"Pick them up and take them home."

I rolled my eyes. *Not now . . .*

"God, they're muddy. I don't want them to ruin my car."

"I *said*, pick them up."

Sometimes all you can really say is, "Yes, Sir."

Sighing, I turned left out of the store parking lot and pulled up alongside them.

"Hop in Bobby, I'll take you home."

As the two climbed into the back seat of my car, I realized it had been nearly a year since I'd heard that "Bring them home" message. I still had no idea what that meant, or even whether my actions had any impact on the two at all. They sat quietly all the way up the street. When I stopped, Sissy jumped out and raced up to the trailer. Bobby stayed put.

"Um . . ." He looked at me in my rear view mirror. "I just wanted to thank you for all you done for us. For talking to her about Jesus. A lot of people make fun of her because she don't go to church. I just wanted to thank you because, you know, even though I gave up on myself, God never gave up on me."

I felt an inch tall, watching him walk across the street and up the path to his trailer.

Sometime soon after that Bobby was taken to the hospital. When I heard, I went right over to sit with Sissy. I spotted her coming out of the waiting room, confusion on her face.

"Sissy, how's Bobby?

She looked at me and responded as calmly as if I'd asked what's for dinner. "Oh, he's dead." She walked past me and out the door.

I crumbled and ran to my office. I didn't want anyone to see me as I burst into tears. My pride reared itself, even then, as I realized I didn't want anyone to know I was bawling my eyes out because the town drunk had died.

But in my heart, I desperately wanted to know, *Did I bring him home, God? Did I do enough?*

I saw Sissy a few weeks later, and hardly recognized her. She looked ten years younger. Some people from the community had taken her from the trailer and helped her find a new place to stay. They cleaned her up, gave her new clothes and dyed her hair back to the beautiful auburn it had been before she met Bobby. Startled, I realized I was watching this clean, happy girl walking down the street with people and laughing, just as I'd pictured her a year earlier. God had brought her to a place of peace and was leading her forward, just as he had promised.

Pondering all Sissy had been through, I could now see my own tidal wave as a strange gift, of sorts. In asking me to help Bobby and Sissy despite my perceived lack of means, God had taught me many things about myself and others. And, in allowing me to go without, he'd strengthened my compassion for those in need.

God isn't going to leave me here. He made me a student, and I'm a good student, so I'll just continue to learn and be content until it's time to move forward.

The next lesson came almost immediately, when I hurt my ankle. It started swelling and became quite painful. Still working two jobs, I had no time for such nonsense, so I went to Pastor Marty that Sunday and asked for prayer. He knelt down and laid hands on my ankle. He stood up and he looked at me and said, "Okay, you're healed."

I moved my ankle in amazement. Just like that? It did feel better, and I remembered his wife's amazing testimony after she'd been prayed over for cancer. I wanted to believe it could be this simple.

"Now Cathy," he continued. "Satan's coming for your healing. I can't tell you when, but the symptoms will come back. When they do, you just stand firm and say, 'Satan, I am healed and you cannot have my healing, and you must leave now in the name of Jesus Christ.'

I didn't quite understand his words. I'd not been taught to pray like that. When I told Bo, he was skeptical, but the ankle felt a heck of a lot better, so who was I to argue?

Back at the diner that week, I found another of what had become many opportunities to chat with Ruby and her daughter Lynn. There weren't many tables in this small-town eatery, so we hung out near the kitchen door during our down times and talked. I often brought up God's continuous blessings on my family, particularly when someone left food at our door, or made it possible for me to pay a bill. I could tell behind those sad, tired eyes, Ruby pondered my reports, but she didn't seem moved in the slightest.

One day as I listened to Ruby again blame her husband for keeping her away from the Lord, I said, "You know, it's not by chance that I'm here. God placed me here for you. He's reaching out to you through me. If you take his hand, he'll lead you and the others will follow."

After a business meeting at work the next day, I stopped at the Dollar General store on my way to the diner. On the knick-knack shelf I found a little bell shaped like a woman wearing a wide, hooped dress. There were no others like it on the shelf.

This is pretty.

I rummaged in my pocket, coming up with a dollar and some change, and bought the bell

While driving on to work I heard the Holy Spirit say, "Give her that bell." The command was undeniably clear.

"Really God? But I like the bell."

A quick picture of my mom with the candle flashed through my mind, pretty much sealing the deal. I stopped at another shop along the way and purchased a card. Before entering the diner, I walked over to Ruby's car, a beat up dodge that she left unlocked, and set the gift on the passenger seat. I wrote in the card, "God is reaching out to you. Take his hand."

When the shift ended, I made sure to leave before Ruby to avoid an awkward scene in the parking lot. For the next two weeks the manager put us on different shifts, but when I entered the diner two weeks later, Ruby came running to me.

"Guess what!"

I couldn't.

"My husband and I went to a revival meeting this weekend and we were both saved!"

Ruby just gushed with excitement. Her cloud of sadness had been lifted. After that, she started going to church, then her kids then her grand kids started attending as well. Three months later, Lynn also gave her life to Christ.

As the fullness of God's plan at the diner came to fruition, I became overwhelmed at his goodness. He had allowed me to see how he carefully orchestrated every moment to bring his people into his kingdom, using those of us who made themselves available for his purposes. Although I'd been pretty much an unwilling partner for most of the journey, as I saw how he'd established my role in helping Bobby and Sissy, and Ruby and Lynn, I felt humbled to realize he had been simultaneously working plans in my own life that would also make more sense in hindsight than they did at that moment.

"I get it, Lord. More trust. I'm trying."

Almost as soon as my "purpose" at the diner had been fulfilled, a job opened up at the Mountain Community Action Programs office (called Mountain CAP). The salary they offered me equaled my current two jobs combined, enabling me to work only one job and see my family more.

The new job signaled the beginning of the end of the tidal wave's initial effects. The waters ebbed and receded to the ocean, and my family experienced another brief quiet season. If I'd known anything about tidal waves, I might have realized the seas were just regrouping for another blow.

As Brandie neared high school graduation in 2005, our different viewpoints created a slight rift in our relationship. I wanted her to follow my path, to pursue an education and become self-sufficient, but she had no desire to attend college. You might say we became slightly vocal over the matter.

Brandie followed her own path, marrying her high school sweetheart, Dewayne, who had joined the Marine Corps. As soon as she graduated, she joined him at his duty station in North Carolina. I watched my little girl transition from attending prom one weekend, to celebrating her wedding the next, to her high school graduation, and then moving far away from me a few weeks later.

It broke my heart to see Brandie leave, as I still saw her as my baby girl in her pigtails, with her teddy bear, Bubba, tucked under her arm. However, over time, as she became a successful wife and mother to our grandson, Haiden, and granddaughter, Adryana, our varied viewpoints mattered less and we patched our relationship.

Home life settled into a comfortable routine, with Ryan in his senior year and Sierra already 9. Ryan and I had bonded closely over the years, despite our occasional differences in opinion. In 2007, When he, too, joined the Marine Corps, my heart ached a bit knowing I would have to watch him leave the nest soon.

I could tell he struggled over leaving, but I knew he'd make a good Marine. I told him the same thing I'd been telling him since he was a sweet young 5-year-old, holding the car door open for me.

"Follow your dreams, Ryan." His eyes told me it wasn't the dream holding him back.

"I'll be here when you return."

The house seemed particularly quiet without Ryan. I missed his enthusiasm for life and his easy-going manner. Although quiet and laid back, he'd been my "problem child," the one who challenged me most. He never wanted to obey the rules, not quite venturing into bad behavior, but usually pushing the limits as far as he could.

Sierra, on the other hand, appreciated advice and usually tried to follow it. Still in love with horses, she wanted to be a jockey. As evidence of her passion, Sierra had taken to heart my advice about saving her money for a horse, and, since the age of 4, she had been banking every bit of birthday money, holiday money and wages earned doing odd jobs. Over the course of five years, she saved more than $700.

In March 2006, we put in the remainder needed and bought Sierra's horse, an old and slow quarter horse named Ridge Runnin' Redford (son of Robert Redford). His color looked like a bay but his papers said he was a blue roan.

We put Ridge Runner's title in Sierra's name. Despite his 17 years, she loved riding him as if he were a racehorse, and he patiently let her do so.

Ridge Runner's upkeep drained our budding savings. Our land, although quite spacious, wasn't set up for a horse, so once again we set aside our plans to build a house. We had to bring in bull dozers to level a lot, then build a barn and put up fences. We had two smaller fields we would alternate him on to feed. His upkeep was expensive. Right from the start we had to get his teeth floated (filed even so he can eat more easily). I had no idea a horse had to go to the dentist! Also, his hooves had been neglected so it took a few months to get his feet back to where they should be and then they required bi-monthly maintenance. His feed included a lot of hay and monthly supplements because we didn't have a large enough field area for him to graze.

Needless to say, we put a lot of money into that horse, but I figured if Sierra was that determined to save money all those years, I wanted to support her.

When she was 12, I took her to Kentucky to the Breyerfest where she met retired jockey, Frankie Lovato, Jr. His jockey camp was scheduled the next month and Sierra wanted to go. I told her if she raised the $400 for registration I would get her there. She helped at a farm cleaning stalls, cleaned houses, and worked odd jobs for the Town of Camden, raising the funds in three weeks.

Some well-meaning people called jockey camp dangerous and stupid, but I saw it as a critical building block for her character. I'd never seen so much passion for a dream—who was I to crush it?

We enrolled her in the camp and she had the time of her life. Frankie even let her borrow his racing silks and tack for a school Social Studies project on jockeys that fall. Her project placed second in the State.

I also took her to Pimlico to watch the Women's Jockey Challenges that took place before the Preakness. The trips to Kentucky and Maryland were costly, though. I had barely enough money for food and gas. Sometimes I just didn't eat. But she made it to the camps, workshops and races and became quite confident. When she grew too tall to be a jockey, it didn't faze her at all.

"I'll just be a veterinarian," she announced.

Even with the horse care, by mid-2007, life's pressures had eased in the Schrader household. Bo continued to battle great pain, but with heavy doses of powerful medication and equally heavy, regular doses of Pastor Marty's wisdom, he managed to divert some of his attention toward prayer and listening for God's plan.

We were by no means wealthy, but my new salary combined with Bo's disability stipend gave us breathing room. In addition to my new job, I continued to work as the county's litter control chairman, and our division won many awards for its contributions to the community. However, the victories seemed hollow.

Sitting in my oversized chair one day in that big, beautiful office, its walls covered with framed degrees and awards, I considered all I'd accomplished and tried to tell myself I'd succeeded. But I couldn't. Despite all the evidence to the contrary, I still felt something was missing. I bowed my head and prayed.

Thank you Lord for getting me to where I wanted to be, now get me out of here.

To anyone who has considered uttering a similar prayer I say, be careful what you ask for. The following month my job was cut to part time and I had to quickly find work elsewhere. I ended up in a manufacturing plant, where I supervised 14 employees in the shipping and receiving departments, preparing paper documents to be scanned into digital format.

Spiritually, my situation must have made me look vulnerable to Satan, because he quickly jumped on the opportunity to shoot an arrow my way.

As I walked across the office one afternoon, my ankle buckled and I fell into my desk. I looked down and saw the swelling had returned.

"So much for healing," I murmured. Then it hit me.

This is what Pastor Marty said would happen!

I stood and said out loud, "Satan, you cannot have my healing! Leave now, in the name of Jesus!"

Instantly, the pain left and the swelling subsided, and it hasn't returned since. I raced home to tell Bo.

From the Remnants

Bo had been pondering the merits of healing prayer since Pastor Marty's wife made her "I'm healed" announcement in front of our congregation. Listening to her story, mine, and quite a few others over the year finally got to him, I guess, because he decided perhaps it was time.

"I'm going forward this Sunday." He spoke so matter-of-factly, it barely registered in my brain until that weekend when Pastor Marty sent out an invitation for healing to the congregation.

Bo stood slowly, grimacing as he turned toward the aisle, and reported to the front of the church.

Pastor Marty looked pleased. I wondered sometimes what he thought as he watched us, dealing with our pain as best we knew how in our human-ness. He and a few other men in the congregation laid hands on Bo and prayed intently for complete healing.

Afterward, Bo said very little as we returned home and resumed our routine. He continued to take his medications for several weeks, until some sort of spiritual light bulb lit up his mind.

"Hey! They laid hands on me for healing but I'm still acting like I'm hurt." Bo stopped taking his meds, cold turkey, which is NOT something I advocate to anyone in a similar position.

A few days later he surprised me, and himself, when he stood and announced, "Cathy, I'm not in pain!"

Our God is just so good.

✗ ✗ ✗ ✗ ✗ ✗

Before we move to how all these trials and lessons played in perfectly with God's plan for my life, I should tell you about one other series of events that occurred during our 18-month tidal wave that nearly sent me into hiding.

Pictures had been flashing across my mind of Jesus standing before me with his arms forming an arc in front of him, as if he were holding something big and round. At first, I saw the scene in black and white, like flickering images on a movie reel. Over the next few days, my perspective changed until I stood in the center. I had no idea what this all meant, so I kept it to myself.

The scene changed abruptly one day as I sat in a meeting, holding an open note pad and listening to someone give what must have been an important talk, but my mind had wandered. Suddenly, I saw the image in color; Jesus, his arms still forming an open circle, looking at me with great, loving intensity. As I watched, the white garment on his arms flowed to the ground, his body became a solid form and where he'd been standing I saw only a building, but with the same shape as if he were standing there.

Thankfully I had no role in the meeting at hand, because I switched my focus to the note pad and started sketching madly. The center seemed to be a sanctuary of sorts, with an ornate, Far East-style copper dome and three rooms on either side. The image actually tilted and turned as I drew, giving me a three-dimensional view. I saw loading docks where his hands had been, one on each side.

And I knew, just *knew*, that this was to be called the Comfort in Christ Center. I hadn't seen the inside and had no clue about its purpose, only that it would contain seven rooms, possibly a reflection of the seven-fold ministry of Jesus, which is described in Isaiah 61:1-3.

Finishing my sketches, I looked up, surprised to see people leaving. The meeting had ended. I stared at the building on my note pad.

What is it, God? Why now? Why me?
And what's next?

He told me nothing more. I prayed for answers in earnest over the next weeks and months, but my primary concerns at the time lie more in keeping my head above the tidal wave. It would be years before more pieces to the puzzle fell into place.

RE-STITCHED

I disliked my job immensely. However, I learned more there about shipping and handling than any human should, unless, of course, God is preparing that human for a purpose that would require such skills.

With Bo's healing, the waves that had once threatened to drown us lessened, settling into an easy rhythm, and our feet finally touched the land. Right about that time, God started whispering a most unusual instruction into my heart. Out of the blue one afternoon, I heard him speak as if he were standing right beside me.

"Cathy, make Teddy bears."

Yeah, right.

The first few times I heard it, I just smiled and shrugged.

I don't think so.

"Make Teddy bears."

Eventually, when I realized it wasn't going to stop, of course I started talking back.

Are you serious? Lord. I don't even know how to sew.

"Make Teddy bears."

I figured God *must* be talking to the wrong person. Why would I want to do that? I thought of the bear I'd clutched that day I returned to Webster. My only comfort that day.

"Comfort in Christ."

Comfort in Christ Bears, now there's a thought...

"Make Teddy bears."

On it went. For nearly a year I tried to run from the idea, but the voice in my heart wouldn't let up.

And, as I've learned and re-learned many times (and as you must have figured out by reading this far in the story), God always gets his way. Since I refused to budge from my "at-last" comfortable life, he decided to move me himself.

One Sunday in the midst of my rebellion, as I dressed for that morning's service at Assembly of God church, a thought penetrated my spirit.

"Go to Compassionate Hope this morning. Read, tell your story, and sing."

The thought came complete with specific readings in the Bible and specific hymns. I knew the scriptures and songs; they lined up perfectly with my story, and I knew that I *could* do what God was asking, but whether I *should* was a completely different issue.

Compassionate Hope was Pastor Steve's church. We'd worked together for a while on the prom dress ministry, but I could hardly even call him a friend at that time... more like an acquaintance.

I can't just take over his service, God. You know I can't do that.

After dressing, I went into the kitchen for breakfast, where the Holy Spirit continued to nudge me. His words rang like a song I couldn't turn off.

"Compassionate Hope, Compassionate Hope, Compassionate Hope."

Pastor Steve doesn't even know me!

I honestly thought I could reason with God.

Besides, it's been months since I last sang in the choir. I'd make a fool of myself.

I jumped into my car to go to church and started the engine. I made it as far as the end of my street, where I looked to the right, preparing to merge with the traffic. Pastor Marty's church was just down the road.

"Go left."

Seriously? I don't want to.

"I *said*, go to Compassionate Hope!"

As I mentioned before, there comes a time when you just have to say, "Yes, Sir."

I turned left.

I sat in my car, parked on the street for about 20 minutes, admiring the tiny white-steepled church with its stained glass window and big blue double doors.

What am I supposed to say to him, God? The pastor's going to think I'm nuts.

God didn't answer. After a while, noting on the marquee that the service would start in half an hour, I figured I'd just go inside and tell the pastor what happened.

Let HIM decide what to do about it. If he shoots me down, I'll stay for the service and then leave, no hurt feelings at all.

I found Pastor Steve working on sound equipment at the back of the church, looking somewhat askance, but he smiled when I approached.

"Cathy, it's good to see you!" He wrapped two hands around my outstretched one and smiled. Encouraged that at least he recognized me, I took a deep breath and just let the words tumble out.

"Okay, I have no idea why, but I felt as if the Holy Spirit told me to come here today and offer to speak. He even told me the exact devotional, testimony, and songs to share. I know you're going to think I'm—"

I stopped when I noticed the grin on Pastor Steve's face.

"What's going on?"

"Well now." He pulled out the day's program and pointed at the order of events. "See this part where it says devotional? I don't have anyone to do that today. And here, where it says testimony, I don't have anyone to do that either. And here? Praise and Worship? I had absolutely no idea who was going to do that until just this minute."

Bewildered, I could only stare as he continued.

"Cathy, everyone who usually helps out around here is gone this week. I've been sitting here praying for someone to come in, so I guess if you're the one God sent to us, we'd better welcome you with open arms, don't you think?"

So I stayed. I'd not attended a church where members of the congregation gave their testimonies that freely, but apparently it was common practice there. I talked briefly about how God had brought me through a valley of personal and financial despair to a point where I could now praise him and trust him again. I couldn't talk about Tiffany and Matthew, as I knew the pain would overwhelm me if I tried, but I thought of them while I talked. After we sang the hymns God had set out for us, the service ended and I sighed deeply.

Thank you Lord. That was good.

I'm sure I only imagined hearing, "I told you so."

One of the ladies in the congregation approached me, dabbing at her eyes with a tissue.

"Thank you." She smiled broadly. "That was exactly what I needed to hear today. I'm so glad you came to visit."

The atmosphere at Compassionate Hope left me electrified. Don't get me wrong, I truly enjoyed listening to Pastor Marty; his analytical approach to the Word of God helped me learn so much, and at a time when I needed to know as much as possible about God. Besides, the healing prayer he'd spoken over Bo had brought such great relief that Bo was nearly ready to start working again. I loved Pastor Marty and everything about his church. However, I felt this new church tugging at me.

I told Bo what had happened and said I was thinking about transferring. He grinned.

"When do we start?"

I sent flowers to Pastor Marty and Alida, explaining the tug I felt and thanking him for all the wisdom and prayer he'd imparted to me and Bo over the years. I don't think either of us would have made it through the darkness without Pastor Marty.

Bo, whose back was now completely healed, entered Compassionate Hope Church with a heightened new enthusiasm for God's healing nature and a passion to pray for others in pain. So great was his faith that he occasionally chided others for leaving a healing prayer session still leaning on their crutches or sucking on throat lozenges for their colds.

"Hey," he'd say, "Jesus said take up your mat and walk! Why are you still using those?"

I had my old Bo back, but even better than before. The most joyful part of witnessing his healing was hearing him laugh. I'd missed it so much.

We loved our new church, but Bo had a special tie to it. We were walking around the grounds one afternoon, and as usual, he said very little. However, I could see the wheels turning, and I knew he was looking at the past. I put my arm through his and whispered.

"Where are you, Bo?"

He seemed somewhat startled to see me there, but gave me a sad smile and walked me over to a stone wall along the sidewalk. We sat, and Bo quietly, almost wistfully, told me his story.

"This was my Dad's church." He glanced up at the white steeple. "He's a bishop now, but his ministry started here, back when I was in high school. I remember going to revivals and being quite active in this church."

I held his hand, waiting until he continued.

"Then one day he just left us. Walked out on my 18th birthday to start his new life. Left me dealing with so much anger I could hardly contain it. I joined the Marine Corps because I had to get away, but the anger followed me. You get plenty of time to stew in the Corps, and I did. Tried to drink it away, but that didn't work either."

Bo had already told me many parts of this story, but I let him talk to see where we were leading.

"When I left the Corps I came back to Webster County. Nowhere else to go, really. I showed up on his front porch one night after I'd been drinking and just let him have it—everything I'd been bottling up for years. I screamed and swore at him until he came out of his house and then I screamed some more."

A hint of realization crept into Bo's face, rising like dawn on a quiet morning.

"Do you know what? Throughout my entire rant, he never raised his voice. Never shouted back. Just let me vent."

Bo cleared his throat.

"Of course, now that I know more, I understand why he left and I don't blame him. At the same time, between some negative events at his church and the rocky relationship with my mom, he almost gave up on being a minister. But when he remarried, his new wife Ann became his greatest supporter. He changed the course of our family, and he turned his life around. And I don't blame him anymore for remarrying. He found a good woman . . ."

Bo turned to face me.

"Cathy, Dad's a good man. A praying man. He prayed for me that night, he and Ann. He said I would always be welcome in his home. I'm sure his prayers kept me from going over the edge when my first wife left, and probably led me to you."

Bo looked up at the church, his eyes misting, then back to me. I hadn't seen this much resolve in him in many years.

"Cathy, I'm going to follow my father's footsteps. I've decided to go into ministry."

х х х х х х

Pastor Steve may not have emphasized the same analytical depth of theology as Pastor Marty, but he more than made up for it with his enthusiastic love for God and in urging us to embrace the power of prayer and outreach ministry. When I told him about God's continued prompting to make Teddy bears, he smiled and nodded, as if it were the most natural request for God to make. In fact, he went out and purchased ten bags of stuffing, which he presented to me after a service.

"Let's make bears!" He beamed so greatly I had to smile back. But I remained unconvinced.

During one of his next sermons Pastor Steve reminded us that sometimes Jesus has to tell us something three times before we stop to listen to him.

I chuckled to think how many times God had made the bear suggestion by that time.

Perhaps he should have used this rule of threes.

But God would have the last laugh.

Compassionate Hope Church

Bo's dad, who started his ministry in this little church on McGraw Ave., eventually moved on to another church. Sadly, under subsequent leadership, its attendance waned, forcing the church to close its doors. Three elderly ladies in the congregation, praying continuously, chipped in to keep the electricity on, believing God had plans to restore the church.

Pastor Steve arrived, excited about a vision he had to restore a church in his wife's home town. However, she had no desire to return. When he told her about the building, she initially said, "I'm sorry, but you're going to have to get a new vision."

The old, vine-covered church looked desolate. Nevertheless, he went inside, where he had to side-step dead birds and piles of filth in the sanctuary. He nearly wept.

"God, this place shouldn't be restored; it needs to be condemned."

But something held him there. He looked out the window at the faceless people passing by, and then at the pool of light the stained glass window created in the center of the floor.

Pastor Steve knelt down in the light and prayed. "God, let me see them through your eyes." He rose and opened the church doors, noticing right away the faces of passersby. He saw tremendous need in their eyes, and his heart filled with compassion.

He was home.

To renovate the church, Pastor Steve relied on prayer for all his needs. Although he raised only $8,000 of the $128,000 needed to build additional classrooms onto the church, he hired contractors to start working. After 12 separate contractors quit before laying the footers, he nearly gave up. However, the thirteenth completed the job. As Pastor Steve was pulling out his checkbook to pay the contractor, the man said, "Don't worry about it; consider it a donation."

A mission team then built the new wing, volunteering all their time and labor. The entire addition cost exactly $8,000.

From the Remnants

At work that week, a co-worker named Connie pulled me aside. "Cathy, I've been clearing out my craft closet, and I have a few odds and ends that I'd hate to throw away. Do you suppose your church's outreach center could use them?"

We did store supplies for community programs and activities, so I didn't hesitate.

"Sure. My car's unlocked. Just toss whatever you have in the back. The latch to the trunk is on the inside. You can put items there as well."

Connie filled my car and trunk to overflowing with remnants of beautiful fabric, spools of ribbon, and bags of stuffing and buttons. The next day she filled it up a second time. I had trouble storing it until I could get to the church. I stuffed as much as I could fit into a giant garden tub that sat inside our trailer, and brought some into the living room, much to Bo's dismay.

Pastor Steve laughed when I told him this story. "Cathy, is God going to have to deliver a third donation before you start listening and make the bears?"

Sure enough, the next day Connie brought more. I added her donations to my growing pile, and just stared at it. Pastor Steve might be onto something. Everything I needed to make bears was overflowing out of the garden tub and all over my bedroom and living room floors.

Uncle!

I had to smile as I prayed.

Okay, God. Yes, Sir. I don't understand what you're up to, but I guess I'm now a bear maker.

I stopped by the town retail store and purchased a basic model sewing machine and a bear pattern. Then I called Carolyn, a friend who knew how to sew. I'd learned through working with her on some community development projects that she sold handmade crafts at local fairs. I asked if she could teach me some basic sewing tips, enough to make a bear at least, and she agreed.

The pattern consisted of four parts, two front and two back, to be sewn together top to bottom. This meant the completed bears would have a seam running down the center in the front and back, and seams down both sides.

For my first bear, I chose an orange, red and yellow fall-ish plaid material, because it looked bright and cheery. Carolyn showed me how to lay the pattern down and pin it to the material then she left me alone to cut it out while she worked on her own project nearby.

I tackled that fabric like a kid with construction paper, snipping right through those pesky little black triangles. It was difficult enough staying on the black line; I wasn't about to veer off course for triangles. Finally, I raised my finished pieces in victory.

"Nice job," said Carolyn. "Now, remove the pattern and pin your material sides together, connecting them at the darts."

"Connect the dots?" I examined the fabric. "What dots?"

"Darts. Those triangle parts that extended outward." Carolyn gave me a patient smile that broadened when she examined my work more closely. "Oh, my. Well, you can work without them; you'll just have to line up the sides carefully."

I put the pieces together as best I could, not understanding the alignment considerations that must be accounted for with plaid patterns. Nothing matched at all.

"All right then, let's give you a quick sewing-machine tutorial," Carolyn said, laughing at my horrified expression. "Don't worry, Cathy, you'll be fine. You should be able to sew this together in about 30 minutes."

I spent the next three and a half hours stitching, backing up, removing, restarting, and re-stitching—laughing and chatting with Carolyn the entire time, because crying wasn't an option. At last I held up a pathetically misaligned hodgepodge of bunched material shaped somewhat like a bear.

Carolyn seemed to be fighting to keep a straight face. "Are you sure God wants you to make these? Honestly, Cathy, you don't have a clue what you're doing!"

She sent me home to practice. Somehow, I remained hopeful. I set up the sewing machine at home, forgetting all Carolyn had taught me earlier about threading the needle. Ryan (who hadn't yet left for boot camp at this time) figured it out right away, the show off.

I plowed forward, cutting (around the darts), matching, and sewing, bear after bear. I argued with that machine constantly, as material bunched up, thread snapped, and knots formed underneath.

How could anyone possibly enjoy this?

From the Remnants

But I kept going. Each bear came out better than the one before. By fall, I'd made nearly 20 bears, and had become somewhat proficient. Still, most of the poor things looked quite amateurish.

So, what do I do with them, God? They're certainly too hideous to sell . . .

A few weeks before a retreat for the women at my church, I had my answer. I'd give them away as door prizes at the retreat.

Nobody can return a door prize.

Despite their many flaws, I liked the bears. They had a simple charm that made me smile. Besides, I'd spent so much of my life working to re-purpose unwanted items, I liked the idea that these bears were made completely from donated remnants. Still, I thought, something's missing. One evening, as I sat quietly in prayer, a poem started forming in my mind. Mind you, I'm not a poet, so this surprised me, and I figured I'd better grab a pen and write it down before I forgot the words. Here's what I heard:

> *My pieces were torn and tattered, cast aside by society.*
> *But Jesus felt I mattered and saw what I could be.*
> *He took my torn pieces and handled them with care.*
> *Sewn together with His love. I've become your teddy bear!*

The beautiful words left me pondering God's strange ways. Not only could he make adorable teddy bears from scraps, through a person who's never sewn in her life, but he does the same with torn and tattered lives.

…Like mine.

I sat up.

Is that what you've been trying to teach me, God?

It made so much sense. He makes beauty with scraps; how much more can he create beauty in our lives from the remnants of what we've been through? Regardless of what we see when we look in the mirror, he knows what we *can* be.

My heart swelled and tears began to run down my cheeks. I tried to pray, but I could only whisper in awe.

Oh God, you really do love me. Thank you for showing me this. And thank you for the beautiful life you've given me.

Now that I understood the bears had a healing purpose, I poured my heart into preparing for the retreat. I copied the poem onto bookmark-like tags, which I tied around the necks of each bear. Then I prepared a short testimony, figuring that if they knew the story of the bears, the women would be more forgiving of their crude state.

At the retreat, although I still couldn't talk about Tiffany and Matthew, I talked about Mom's candle, and our financial story, and Bobby and Sissy, as well as all the experiences God led me through to bring me to this point.

"Bottom line," I concluded. "If God tells you to do something, don't wonder why; just do it."

The testimony seemed to hit home, and the women loved their bears. My work was finished . . . or so I thought.

Almost immediately, orders for more bears started pouring in. Women who didn't receive a bear at the retreat asked if I'd make them one. Women who *did* receive bears wanted more so they could give them to other people they knew who were suffering from various heartaches.

Regardless of what I'd believed was the message of my talk, they'd heard something else entirely: that God could turn their lives around as well. The bears represented hope for those who couldn't imagine how God would make anything of the mess they were in.

As word spread and bear orders piled up, I hired Connie, who had kicked this project off with her donation, to help me sew. Having an employee meant being responsible for another person's paycheck, so I stumbled through the process of becoming a limited liability corporation, which required registering with the state.

Before I knew what hit me, I was in the bear business.

I called the business Comfort in Christ Bears, remembering the phrase I'd heard when God told me about the ministry that would be built one day. . . not by me, of course, but perhaps I'd be part of it.

Meanwhile, Bo, eager to get back into the workforce after four years away, found a job at a grocery store. Although he made less than before, the work gave him an opportunity to build his strength and re-enter the daily grind gradually. He discovered that one of the most stressful parts of being healed is *stopping* a disability stipend. Apparently, Federal government workers are unaccustomed to receiving such requests. It took a bit of stubborn persistence, but Bo finally succeeded, and the disability payments ended.

The bear business gained traction, but hardly made money. For one thing, I couldn't charge much for the bears, considering the depressed economy in West Virginia. I found similar bears being sold on the internet for around $50, but it wasn't about the money. It was about the message, God's message of hope and healing. I settled on $30.

However, and for another thing, I gave many bears away. God reminded me continuously of the day I'd stood on that porch, having lost everything. My purpose, and the bears' purpose, was to help people who had suffered loss.

I gave them away to women, mostly, whether they were going through divorce, had lost children or loved ones, or were gravely ill or even dying. The bears brought hope. To victims of rape or abuse, they said, "You may be broken, but you're not shattered. God can piece you together." I liked to believe God was giving them the bears, providing desperately hurting women the same life-changing moment he'd given me.

"You can't keep doing this," Connie said. "You're running a business; you can't just give away inventory."

I'd try, but whenever I saw a need, I donated a bear, reasoning that it's not as if I'd spent money on the supplies. Then, as the initial pile of materials dwindled and I realized I'd either have to solicit more or purchase some, I made more of an effort to charge for them.

One day I received a flannel hoodie shirt in the mail. It had belonged to a teenage boy named Steve who died unexpectedly. His heartbroken mother sent me the shirt, asking if I could make it into a bear, saying her grief counselor had told her about me, and thought having such a memento might help her heal.

Filled with compassion for the sweet woman, I accepted the job right away. I laid the template on the flannel and cut out the pattern. After sewing and stuffing the bear, I used the shirt buttons for his eyes and tied the hoodie string in a bow around his neck. He looked adorable, if I do say so myself.

I gave the leftover material to a friend, who made three flannel ornaments from it, and we sent those to his mom as well. She gave them to three of his grieving friends as mementos of their lost buddy.

Not long afterward, I received a note from the woman.

Cathy, Our Steve Bear arrived today and gave me a big hug! I love him, and I love you for doing this. Of course, my tears flowed; but what a blessing. Even though I knew our Steve Bear was coming, it really gave me a warm feeling to see him today and to have him here. I love his little collar too! When I run my fingers along the collar to straighten it, I can almost hear my son saying, "Mom, it's ok, I'm fine!"

Thank you from the bottom of our hearts. You did a wonderful job, Cathy, bless you.

My eyes filled with tears as I read the note. What joy I felt to know that one of these simple bears could bring comfort to a grieving mother.

✗ ✗ ✗ ✗ ✗

Between the equine expenses and bear giveaways, I had little money to myself. However, one afternoon while sitting alone in the house and flipping through the television channels, I came across Daystar Television Network in the middle of their spring fund-raising share-a-thon. Their special guest, John Hagee of Christians United for Israel, along with Marcus and Joni Lamb, were encouraging people to donate to help build the Daystar Trauma Care Unit. The wing would be added to the Assaf Harofeh Medical Center, east of Tel Aviv.

The announcer dared listeners to take part in the $1,000 pledge challenge, asking us to consider making either the $1,000 lump sum payment or split their donations into $84 payments over the course of a year.

"Pledge $1,000, Cathy."

Oh dear, not again.

Even though I had heard God's instructions many times and knew his voice, I still debated with him.

Lord, you know I don't have the money to do that!

I even dialed a few friends, hoping they'd talk me out of it. However, no one answered their phones.

Okay God, I'll make the pledge but you'll have to pay the $84 each month.

Despite the risk, I made the pledge as a donation from Comfort in Christ Ministries, and God responded faithfully. I sold enough bears every month to make the payments. Today, a plaque for Comfort in Christ Ministries is on display in the trauma wing.

As my business grew, it soon became apparent I needed more publicity to reach beyond Webster Springs' borders, so I created brochures and started a website. More orders came in, making me wonder if I'd grown too quickly. I needed more help, more materials, and better technology.

At the time, I'd been hand-cutting all my patterns. For every 100 bears I had to cut 400 pieces. I just couldn't keep up. I knew a die-cut press would help, but I didn't have the money to buy one.

You got me into this, God, I prayed. *How do you suppose you're going to supply a press?*

Almost immediately, I came across the Hello Tomorrow Fund contest sponsored by Avon on the internet for women in business, which awarded a weekly prize (for 13 weeks) to women whose businesses made a positive impact in their community. The prize amount? Naturally, it was $5,000—just what I needed to purchase a press and die cut plates.

There's no way I'll win. I'm barely a business yet.

I couldn't imagine what they'd see in my fledgling start-up. However, I decided I had nothing to lose.

I already don't have the money anyway.

Despite my disbelief, I filled out the application describing my new business and its healing, uplifting mission, as well as my need for a die-cut press. I also wrote of its potential to create work for many women in our impoverished community. Then I dropped it in the mail. I barely thought about it after that, until a letter arrived informing me that of the 1,250 applicants, my business had been named one of 29 finalists in the program.

It floored me to think the judges—including some prominent business women like Sarah Ferguson, Duchess of York; Phylicia Rashad; and Suze Orman—were examining my application and assessing my business' future potential. It floored me once again when I learned that I'd been selected as one of the winners! Who could have guessed?

Oh, right, God would.

As soon as the money arrived, I bought the press and got to work, praising God for his constant provision.

People started requesting smaller bears, which turned out to be a blessing as well, because the original 18-inch pattern wouldn't fit the press. I went to the Robert C. Byrd Institute at Marshall University, where some staff members helped me condense my pattern on the computer and create smaller plates.

In addition to helping me acquire the press and increasing the business' name recognition, winning that contest kicked off a season of growth during which every success seemed to lead to yet another. For example, a Christian catalog company contacted me after reading a newspaper article about the Avon award and offered to carry the bears for retail, saying they'd be featured in the fall catalog. I accepted their proposal and sent off my application without even stopping to think about it, or worse, to pray about it. How could I, at the rate changes were occurring?

When I told Bo, he seemed skeptical.

"Have you looked into this company?" He wasn't trying to dissuade me, but merely make me do my homework.

"I haven't, but it's a Christian company." I gave him a quick shrug as I headed out the door. "Besides, *they* came to *me*. I'm pretty sure it will be okay."

TANGLED THREADS

"It's here! It's here!" I slammed the mailbox shut and rushed into the house balancing the mail and my bags in one arm while waving a magazine above my head with the other. I set my bags on the couch and joined Bo and Ryan in the kitchen.

"My bears are now officially on the national market!" I held the catalog in front of me with two hands so they could take it in. "That's right, check out that front cover!"

I set the catalog on the table. Although the text on the cover said only "Holiday 2009," the red and green theme did set a Christmas tone: Under a large green wreath, three mitten-clad children and a big Labrador retriever gathered around a sled. One girl of about 9 or so held a festive green wicker basket, in which sat a large, poinsettia-patterned Comfort in Christ bear.

"Oh, it's so charming!" I started leafing through the pages for the description. I couldn't find it in the Encouraging Gifts sections, and they didn't seem to have a Faith section. Bo spotted it first.

"Here it is, Cathy, with the toys."

"Toys? But it's not a toy. . . well, I guess. . ."

From the Remnants

There he sat, a different bear from the one on the cover, this one a multi-colored checker-print bear, among a group of stuffed animals. My message of hope was sharing space with a pig, a rabbit, and an octopus. To add insult, the narrative beside it read, "Comfort Bear" instead of "Comfort in Christ Bear."

Amid the disappointment, I couldn't stop staring at the bear. Something else was wrong. At first, I couldn't quite place it. I studied the brightly colored bear in the photo. He was mine, all right, from his dark triangle nose to the white satin bow tied around his neck.

His neck...that's it!

"Oh no! They took off the tag! The poem!" A wave of betrayal washed over me.

This can't be happening.

I looked at Bo, fighting back the lump rising in my throat. "That poem gives the bear purpose. It makes these different from ordinary craft bears."

The poem wasn't included in the description, either.

How would customers even know about it?

I checked through the pages again.

Perhaps the bear is somewhere else. A Get Well section, maybe?

Nope. It was just a toy. I stared at the tag-less bear.

"It's almost as if. . ."

"As if they removed all the Christ parts?" Bo took the catalog and examined some of the other products. None seemed to advocate any Christian message.

"But they're a Christian company!" The tears I'd held back made their way out. "Why would they want to do that?"

Bo shook his head. "I don't know, but it's still a nice bear. You'll probably make some sales anyway."

He was right. Over the next few months I received a few orders that I filled myself. I honestly don't think I could have handled any more than a few.

However, I did contact the catalog company to explain the errors. They never corrected them; the bears remained tag-less, "Comfort Bears" in subsequent issues. In addition, the marketing company that produced the catalog had increased the price of my bears to grow their profit margin, which I think made them too expensive. This turned out to be a blessing, though, because it limited the scope of yet another disaster that was looming on my horizon, this time, of my own making.

Aside from the catalog, my business continued to thrive. A few months earlier, I'd had the opportunity to experience the bears' true healing potential through the eyes of 30 area foster children, and now doors were opening in that area as well.

I'd known about the foster family children's camp in nearby Beckley for many years through my work in the community. I contacted the camp directors about providing bears to their next group of campers. They loved the idea, considering how many foster children remember their experiences of great heartache and loss.

We made a bear for each child, and found sponsors among the congregations of Beckley's churches to finance the bears and write messages of hope on the back of the tags. I attended the presentation event, and could barely hold back my emotions when I saw the smiles on those children's faces. Children of all ages were clutching their bears tightly, and I saw many happy tears that day.

The event also tugged at my still-open wound. My heart ached as I watched all those children, many of whom were as old as Tiffany and Matthew would have been. I wondered how many of these precious children blamed God for taking their parents.

How many people around the world see God as this great, uncaring father who takes away?

The question startled me.

Do I still see him that way?

I didn't think so, considering all he'd taught me over the past few years, and all the doors he had opened before me, but I knew, deep in my heart, pain lurked.

As we handed out bears, the camp director could barely contain his *own* joy.

"This is a fantastic program you've got here, Cathy. I see smiles on faces that have been scowling since the kids arrived. The healing potential here is monumental."

He thought for a minute before continuing. "You know, Cathy, our company sends about 7,000 kids to camp around the world every year.

I wonder if our international board might be interested in purchasing bears to give away at other camps."

Just the thought set me reeling. I had to lean on my car to keep from falling over.

"I'm not sure . . . How does one even take the first step in an endeavor of such magnitude?"

His face lit up like a street light. "Perhaps you could make a documentary about what the bears are doing for the kids in this camp. I know someone who could film it and put it on CD. Then I could take it to the board.

Still riding the wave of momentum, I agreed. We went to a state park to shoot the documentary. I liked the videographer, a young man whose wife was expecting a baby.

Wow, shipping out of the country? Do I need to learn about costs and regulations?

Life continued to move at blazing speeds. It seemed every time Bo and I had a chance to sit down and discuss the business, I had heaps of new information to lay in his lap.

"Great news, Bo." I handed him a copy of the latest catalog. "The bears are now in thousands of catalogs across the nation. I've already received 33 orders this time, which I have to get out before Christmas."

Bo looked at me thoughtfully. "Have you done any research on the company yet?"

"Stop worrying. It's fine." I shrugged. "Oh, and when this new video is complete, I could get as many as 7,000 new orders from, get this, *around the world!*"

He sighed a long, patience-gathering sigh. I knew he was weighing my joy against his cautious nature. He didn't want to burst my bubble, but he also wanted to protect me.

"Cathy, how are you going to fill 7,000 camp orders and still take care of catalog sales?"

"Oh, I've got that figured out. I'm hiring a company to help. I found them on the internet and they're located nearby."

"The internet?" He arched an eyebrow. "Did you research *that* company? Did they provide references?"

"No, but I met with them last week and they're so nice. We even held a class for the staff, and showed them how to make the bears properly. I got to see them work – all the bears came out perfect! Besides, they handle Federal contracts, so I'm sure they're okay."

"I don't know Cathy." A frown creased Bo's forehead. "You might want to think about slowing down, just a bit. Decisions like this should be made methodically, with research and prayer. Have you prayed about it?"

I can't stand it when he gets logical.

"Yes, I prayed, Bo, but I've been so overwhelmed with all these doors opening that I'm not sure I heard God in all the noise. Besides, for all I know, this could be God opening the doors *for* me."

Inside though, my confidence waned. I didn't have a solid team handling my administration. I ran everything and made every decision. At one point I created a business plan, which I submitted to the Small Business Administration for review. They weren't impressed with the Christian message of hope, or that I called it a "God thing." They only focused on the business aspect of my proposal, and they offered a single bit of feedback:

"You need to charge more for the product."

And, as if the pace of my life weren't busy enough, I also teamed up with three ladies in real estate to open an artisan co-op on Main Street. We received grant funding because of our focus on helping women from the community. Women with all types of artistic talent could come to the shop to learn new crafts and business strategies to market their crafts, and they could share shelf space for selling their crafts in our shop. Setting up the co-op gave me a sense of purpose and accomplishment. I so enjoyed helping women find their way, in part because of the women who had helped me find my way back to the Lord all those years earlier.

My supervisors suggested I put a few bears on display to show the women who signed on that I shared their enthusiasm for creativity and had a vested interest in the co-op. Although I would later sell a few bears through that venue, they were mostly for display purposes. I found more joy in helping other women succeed than in pushing the bears, which were already selling through the catalog and by word-of-mouth.

We'd scheduled the co-op grand opening for October. I could hardly wait!

From the Remnants

Yes, life kept me busy, between the business, my regular job with the county, Bo back at work, and Sierra's hectic school schedule, but I loved every bit of it. With the camp documentary nearly complete and the camp director eager to send the story international, an entire company building bears to meet my catalog orders, and a grand opening scheduled for the co-op, I was on top of the world.

Of course, there was one tiny issue. God, although I'm sure he intended for me to succeed, hadn't exactly intended for me to be spiraling outward at such a dizzying rate.

I'd lost sight of *his* plan for the bears—a little detail he was about to bring to my attention.

UNRAVELED

"Oh, this is just like Christmas!"

I sliced through the packing tape with my box cutter, my hands shaking and my heart ready to sing. Only two thin cardboard flaps lie between me and my first 33 subcontracted bears. As the bears gained popularity, the possibilities ahead seemed endless. I imagined a partnership with this company that could create jobs for many women in our community.

Lifting the flap, I pushed aside the white tissue paper to peer inside. Two tiny black eyes peered back. I could barely contain my giggles as I pulled the first bear from the pile.

"Well, hello Sir. How are y—" I stopped short, noticing that one ear was lower than the other and lop-sided, as if whoever had sewn it had rushed through the task. I certainly couldn't send *this* one to a customer.

I pulled out another bear, whose torso twisted strangely to one side. He looked as if he'd been through a tornado.

Panic started rising in my chest as I pulled out the rest of the order. Every. Single. Bear. Was. Wrong.

From the Remnants

Misaligned seams, crooked arms, legs so badly twisted the bears couldn't sit. Most of the logos on the bears' feet had been sewn on sideways or upside down. The stuffing had been crammed so tightly it looked like rocks. I tried to stay positive.

Perhaps I can salvage them.

But, no. They were not only unfit for sale, they were ruined beyond repair. I ripped each one open, yanked out the stuffing and threw the rest away.

I called the company, but apparently, quality concerns hadn't been addressed in the contract. Not their problem. Adding to the insult, I had to pay for them because I couldn't afford the court costs it would take to fight the company.

Every fiber of my being wanted to lash out and then shut down, but I couldn't. I had to regroup and figure out a way to fill 33 bear orders in under five days.

Two women at the bank who believed in my bear business helped me take out a loan against my new press for $5,000 to pay for the ruined batch, and to cover the cost of making new ones. Essentially, I'd be paying for the same bears twice. I recruited Connie and a few other friends I knew who could sew quickly. It takes about two hours to pin, cut, sew, stuff, finish, and pack one bear for shipping. We sewed 33 bears, barely making the Christmas deadline.

The experience nearly broke me, but I learned some valuable lessons. I didn't have to tell Bo he'd been right about being cautious, and he, bless his heart, didn't gloat.

Resolved to keep my head up, I turned all my energy to the co-op, which, throughout my battle with the subcontractors had been progressing nicely as opening day neared.

I went to the shop one afternoon to check on progress. The quaint little shop, housed in the old drug store on Main Street, offered many nooks and corners for artisans to set up their crafts. I still marveled at how many different kinds of crafts were represented, and that we already had a scrapbook class scheduled for our training area.

The co-op provided hope for many area artisans. Women were thrilled to finally have a place to not only sell some of their work but also interact with like-minded artists. Their talents varied, yet complemented each other. My partners and I were already envisioning ways to combine skills to support events like weddings. We could easily imagine a prospective bride finding just about everything she'd need there for her special day – invitations, decorations, jewelry, mementos to give as gifts, and even a dress or two from the seamstress who had taken a corner stall.

The best thing about the co-op, I thought, was that it belonged to the community. I saw my role as an encourager and a confidence builder. It felt wonderful to see so many women, some initially shy or withdrawn, blossom as they realized they are not only talented, but could actually make a profit from their handicrafts.

Thank you, God, for arranging the grant for this project. I'm sure the backers will be pleased with what we've done.

I giggled when I spotted one of my bears on a shelf, finding it still hard to believe how far I'd come. Who would have thought, considering my first days of working with Carolyn, that these extraordinarily talented women would count me—the woman who just a short time ago couldn't sew a straight line to save my life—among them as a fellow artisan?

"Heading over to the post office," I said to one of my partners. I stepped out of the co-op onto Main Street. The crisp cool air reminded me that winter was on its way. Between preparing for the co-op opening and dealing with the catalog fiasco, I'd had little time to stew over my recent disappointment regarding the camp documentary. Mike, the videographer, had called a few weeks back to tell me he had to pull out of the project. His newborn daughter had arrived prematurely and was experiencing serious health issues that were clearly more important than a documentary.

Though disappointed, I totally understood and supported his decision.

No documentary, no international market.

"I'm fine with that, God." I smiled upward. "I guess I'll be happy with national sales for now."

Surely, although I hadn't exactly prayed about my recent business decisions, I had God's approval. The bears were his idea anyway, right? And besides, at least half of what I made from bear sales would go right back into making more bears or to fund charities.

After I pay off that darned $5,000 loan, that is.

I entered the post office, which was only moderately busy, and stepped into line behind an acquaintance I'd worked with on many projects through my community development job. We started chatting about the co-op.

Well, to be precise, I suppose, I chatted. She stood statue-still, staring at the front of the line.

"It's all so exciting," I gushed, pulling out a flier one of the co-op women had drafted. "We're going to have our grand opening on the same day as the chili cook-off. That way we might bring in some of the people in town for the festival. I'll be putting this on as many windows as I can."

The woman ignored the paper, turned her icy cold eyes in my direction, and said, "You know, no one wants you here."

What?

My mind reeled at her words. My entire *body* reeled, as if I'd received an electric shock. She walked away, leaving me staring at her retreating form with my mouth open.

Where did that come from?

In that moment I received my first hint about a storm that had been brewing behind the scenes, apparently for quite some time. I learned over the next weeks that some people perceived our co-op to be a threat to other businesses in town. Frankly, I never did quite understand their reasoning, because our co-op offered unique, handmade crafts that couldn't be obtained elsewhere, and unique services like marketing and small business classes. I had tried very hard not to bring in the same types of art work the other shops sold. When I approached people to join our co-op I never asked them to leave the other shops. If they already had an outlet for their crafts I left it alone and moved on to others who might not have the same opportunity. The established shops were filled to overflowing and had no room to accept new artisans.

However, my view turned out to be irrelevant. Someone filed a complaint, and we received notice that we couldn't advertise our grand opening because a committee would be looking into the claim. Some of our women left the co-op during the episode, whether to avoid the drama or because they believed the allegations, I'll never know. All I knew for sure was that our once-beautiful entryway now lay bare.

Three days before the grand opening, I found myself staring ruefully at the bare corner shelves in the entryway, trying to decide what to put there. That's when Shannon, one of my partner's sisters, entered the co-op with a basket full of odds and ends.

"I heard you could use some more crafts." She set the basket on a bench with an apologetic shrug. "These aren't very good and I don't know what you'll do with them, but you can use them if you like."

Reaching into the basket, I pulled out a lovely garland made from material remnants and a snowman ornament she had fashioned out of a tin can lid.

"Shannon, these are gorgeous!"

She shrugged again, but I could see she was pleased. "Just something to do while I watch the kids play ball."

The basket held several treasures, each of which re-purposed items that just about anyone else would have considered trash. We put a small Christmas tree in the corner and decorated it with the garland and ornaments. When I stood back, I could barely contain my joy.

"Shannon, you're amazing. I do believe you've saved the store."

> *In the years to come, Shannon and her sister would eventually buy the building that housed the co-op and convert it into a thriving little country store. Despite all the turmoil of the times, I'll always smile when I remember her first steps, taking a chance that turned a simple hobby into a business.*
>
> *As with Shannon's story, the co-op didn't make a lot of money, but it changed many lives. Linda, who created lovely hand-made jewelry, came to me despondent one day because her sales couldn't quite meet her family's needs. I knew about a job opening in town and encouraged her to apply. She was not only hired but last I checked still worked there.*
>
> *Also, my friend Loren, the counselor who had given us money when Bo's back went out, lost her job just when we needed extra help at the co-op and so she volunteered. Before long, she started selling her jewelry and then expanded into other products like candles and incense. Eventually, she took her work out of the co-op and made some good money, selling at area craft shows.*

From the Remnants

Because of the no-advertising directive, our grand opening came and went with little fanfare. A few weeks later, local authorities determined that the co-op violated no regulations.

Sadly, whoever had been behind the complaints wasn't satisfied and decided to go after me personally. In February, I received a letter in the mail notifying me of a pending investigation by the ethics committee for my alleged conflict of interest. Reportedly, I'd solicited and accepted grant money for a project that enabled me to sell my bears.

The sting of that letter nearly crushed me. Not only were the allegations false, but they attacked my ministry and my character.

To make matters worse, these were people who *knew* me. They had worked with me for years. They knew I wouldn't purposely do anything to violate rules or be manipulative. This cold, senseless stab in the back shook me to the core.

The university, which had contributed some of the grant funding, saw no breach of ethics, and they even fought my case, successfully proving that the bears weren't generating income through the shop. Although I beat the allegations, the university asked me to pull down the bears to avoid perceived conflict of interest.

None of that mattered though. The remaining grant supporters pulled their co-op funding.

After this blow I lost my desire to help the town and allowed my work to falter. My job, funded through three different venues, lost one of its backers when they decided not to renew my position. The other two could not carry the difference and I was given notice that my job would be ending. My boss called me in and told me I should start looking for work elsewhere.

I honestly felt no bitterness by that point; I barely felt anything at all. I thanked my boss and said, "This makes things easier. You've just forced me to move."

By the end of 2010, I was left again with nothing. Not even meeting with Chris for lunch could lift my spirit.

"You'll be okay, and life will go on. . . unlike the people in Humongous."

The mischievous glint in his eye reminded me of the terror I'd felt after watching that movie with him when we'd been teenagers. The movie, about a creature named Humongous, had been frightfully dark, in more ways than one. It left us on edge for a few days, particularly near the water. One afternoon we'd taken his canoe up river to the general store and come home so late shadows had cast an eerie darkness across the river. Our canoe became lodged in a rock, and we had to climb into the dark water to release it. Chris chose that moment to shout, "Humongous! There! In the water behind you!"

His eyes continued to smile, telling me he'd been remembering my terrified scream.

"I can't Chris. I can't laugh at that now. I don't think I'll ever laugh again." I'd not eaten in days, yet the plate of food in front of me held little appeal.

Chris took a bite of his sandwich and stared at me with intense compassion while he chewed. He paused before taking another bite.

"I'm worried about you." His eyes had lost their twinkle. "The Cathy I know is a relentless fighter. She wouldn't let something like this stop her."

"Yes, well, the Cathy you knew cared about people." I felt the familiar trembling sobs making their way up from my heart. "This Cathy has been beat up too much. She has no desire to help anymore."

TAILOR MADE

"If God calls you to do something, Satan will try to steal it." Mom's adage swirled around my heart, but I'd already started piling up the bricks.

When it comes to the bears, God, you can have them.

The sheer weight of my grief practically paralyzed me toward the end of 2010. Even after all the time God had invested in showing me his goodness and teaching me to step out in obedience despite having no idea what he was up to, I still hadn't learned to trust that God had my best interests at heart.

In many ways, I felt as if I were standing back on that porch, devastated, disheartened, and lost in disbelief.

Why would you allow this, God? I thought I was following you. I thought I was making the right decisions.

The source of my devastation was not the failure. I'd become accustomed to falling down. I'd tried many things and failed, fallen and always managed to stand back up. This time was different, because I'd been betrayed by people I'd known, worked with, and trusted for years.

. . . and I've lost my ministry.

From the Remnants

"No, you haven't," Bo would say. "God has simply stripped away everything other people were attaching to it. You have to get up and start again."

I refused to listen to him. I did notice that some aspects of my grief affected me differently this time around. I'd learned enough about God's sovereignty that, rather than become angry at him, I lost my confidence in my own decision making. I began to doubt I was actually discerning God's will. That bold woman who only a year ago had delighted in saying "Okay God, I don't understand where this is going, but since you said it, I'll do it" now sat like a turtle in its shell, afraid to move for fear of making a mistake.

I let the devastation take me to the ground, and I didn't care about standing again. Opportunities arose, but they made me leery. I'd ponder them, and offer the Lord only sarcasm.

Sure, God. Remember when I took that leap of faith off the cliff? Remember when you didn't catch me? No way I'm doing that again.

I stopped making payments on the loan I'd taken against the press.

What's the point of paying for something I'll never use?

When the bank came to repossess my press, I felt awful knowing I'd let down the women who had helped me get that loan. As I watched the repo man load the heavy contraption onto his truck, I lamented its significance as the end of a ministry that *almost* made it off the ground.

"You know," I said, "God uses the torn pieces of our lives to put our lives back together." I ran my hand over its smooth metal frame. "Perhaps one day he'll put this ministry back together."

The man slid the machine into the truck bed then stepped back to stare at it with me. "I believe he will," he said. Then he closed and locked the heavy sliding door, jumped into the cab, and drove away.

Bo found me sitting at the kitchen table, sobbing over a cup of coffee. He said nothing, but walked to my chair and stood behind me, gently massaging my shoulders. I turned and rose, falling into his arms, where he held me and let me cry some more. This, too, represented a change from my previous grieving period. I told him about the press and what the man had said.

"But it doesn't matter. It's over, Bo." I sank back into the chair. "I can't keep the ministry going."

Bo poured himself a cup of coffee and sat across from me.

"Cathy, it doesn't have to be over." He put a hand on mine, waiting until I looked into his eyes. "You have a bear pattern, a sewing machine and a calling. That hasn't changed. Get up. You know God will help you."

I looked away. Part of me wanted to believe him, but that would require the turtle to extend its neck just a little too far.

"I'm not going through this again. My heart can't handle any more disappointment."

Bo got up and grabbed his coat, stopping to kiss my forehead. "I have to go to work, Cathy. You hang in there. And pray. There's an answer here somewhere."

I watched him leave and considered his words, smiling at how similar his encouragement had been to what I'd been hearing from the Holy Spirit.

*Or *think* you've been hearing? There's a difference.*

There had been a recurring theme of encouragement during my attempted prayer time.

Get up and start over. This is not the end of your story. It's the pinnacle, the turning point.

I could almost hear God asking if I intended to let defeat keep me from the hope and future Jesus had promised, or if I would rise and start again?

Defeat, please, if you don't mind.

I was still clinging stubbornly to my sadness the next day when the paperwork for my business license renewal arrived in the mail.

You've got to be kidding me.

As anger welled within me, I hastily grabbed a pen and scrawled across the page, "Out of Business!"

I'm SO done with the bears!

But God was not. And he told me as much, again using Pastor Steve's Rule of Threes.

He began with the license application. As soon as I finished scrawling across it, I stuffed it in an envelope and tossed it into the outgoing mail pile.

"Get it out of there."

I know I heard those words. They rang through my brain as clear as a bell. For whatever reason, I knew implicitly that God wanted me

From the Remnants

to keep the license. So I pulled it out and set it on my desk. I'd deal with it later. If I renewed and paid for the license, I also had to pay my liability insurance.

God didn't seem the slightest bit ruffled by my bitterness. In fact, I think he may have been smiling at me, because in the next few seconds, the phone rang.

"Hello, Mrs. Schrader? Are you the lady who makes teddy bears?"

"Yes I am." I sighed and prepared to tell her I was closing up shop, but she spoke first.

"Well Honey, I am calling you from Chattanooga, Tennessee. My mother passed away almost a year ago and we are just now going through her belongings. We found boxes of material with a cut out picture of you taped to the top of them. I guess she believed in what you were doing with those teddy bears and meant to send it to you, but she passed away before she got the chance. If you'll give me your address, we have boxes of material coming your way."

I looked up and said silently, *Seriously, what part of 'I quit' do you not understand?*

"And Hon?" The woman's voice softened. "You have no idea the lives you are touching with those bears. You keep your chin up, and keep going, okay?"

Speechless, I nodded and hung up the phone.

The bank called the next day and told me to come pick up the press. Apparently, some "angel" investors had taken care of the back payments. Taking it back meant I'd still have to make payments on it for three more years, but I knew this was another of God's behind-the-scenes nudgings, so I arranged to retrieve it.

You know, God, that's going to mean a lot of money heading out but not a whole lot coming in. Even if I were to start again, and I'm not saying I will—do you hear me? Even if I wanted to, I don't have enough material and supplies.

A thought blasted through me like a bolt of lightning, leaving me humbled anew at God's ways. He'd hit me three times again.

I pulled the business license toward me and reached in the desk drawer for a bottle of correction fluid. I dipped and dabbed and painted until the scrawled message faded into the background. Then I filled out the form and a check to go with it.

Cathy Schrader

I can't believe I'm back in the bear business.

Despite that oddly orchestrated Day of Threes, it would be another year or so before I would feel like I could breathe again.

The bear ministry may have survived, but I was forced to let it hibernate while I brought my life back into order. Just as the money from my county job ran out, an opportunity opened for a position with the regional Girl Scouts headquarters in Charleston. Although I wanted to leap at the offer, we had Ryan to consider.

Ryan was expected to come home on leave from the Marine Corps that February—he'd spent time in both Iraq and Afghanistan. Bo and I worried about possible effects of post-traumatic stress, and in reading about ways to mitigate symptoms, we learned it's best not to make major changes for him to return to. One might consider moving to Charleston more than a minor change. We told him of the move, of course, but we wanted to spare him the initial shock of coming home to unfamiliar surroundings.

Aside from that, Bo and I both thought moving would be a good idea. Bo felt ready to move up from the grocery store job to something more challenging. Without pain in his back, he had even resumed some outdoor activity. It made my heart glad to hear him laughing outside while he played basketball with our grandson.

So, I accepted the position in Charleston and went ahead of the family, leaving Bo to help Ryan settle back into a routine. The set-up worked well, as I was able to stabilize in my new job and search for a place for us to live. I stayed with Brian and his family during that time, for about six weeks.

It seemed strange chatting with Brian without Chris nearby, but we had some good talks. Brian spoke openly about his relationship with Chris, as well as his faith. I could see his confusion as he weighed the two.

Although Chris and Brian had been together since college, their lives had not been without struggle and pain. Chris had entered into a period of darkness, emotionally and financially. He had a good job and made plenty of money, but it all seemed to go down the drain. I also suspected Brian had moved back home to give Chris some space, but it wasn't my business, so I didn't ask.

"It kills me to see him unhappy," I told Brian. "I wish I could help. He's always been there for me, and I do know how he can find peace, but there are some things he just won't hear, and I can't make him listen."

Brian looked out the window, tapping his foot restlessly.

"We know, Cathy." He turned to face me, and I winced to see the burden and conflict warring within him. "It's not going to get better until we turn it over to God."

I found an apartment about 20 minutes outside Charleston, in Scott Depot, WV, and started moving our belongings from Webster Springs. I moved everything except primary furniture so Ryan's "home" would continue to look the same. I even lugged the 600-pound press to the new digs. It went immediately into a storage locker, as did the boxes of material.

I also brought the marker for Tiffany and Matthew that had stood at the base of their tree. I couldn't leave it behind.

When Bo joined me, he took a job at a nearby manufacturing plant, where he still works today. Right away we looked for our new home church.

We chose the Tabernacle of Praise in Culloden, a small town outside the city, because Bo had been close to completing the requirements for ordination and would be able to continue his program there. We looked at a few others, but they didn't have vibrant youth groups, which was important to us, considering Sierra was now 14. When we found Tabernacle of Praise, Sierra's the one really who latched on first, because the youth group greeted her so warmly.

I enjoyed listening to our new leader, Pastor Bryan. His calming presence and clear way of talking about the Lord made God's mysterious ways seem logical. When I told him about my bear ministry disaster and how discouraged I'd become, he just smiled.

"Cathy, with every ministry there is a birth, a crucifixion, and a death. God will resurrect it, in his time and for his glory. Wait on him, and you'll know what to do when he's ready."

I considered Bo's words about the business being pruned of those things God didn't want attached. Perhaps he hadn't intended for it to make great profit, or to gain publicity so quickly. After all, its original purpose had been to reuse scraps and to bless people who were suffering.

Still, although I kept the business alive by paying required fees and continuing to make the payments on the press, I made few bears over the next year or so. One here and one there, when someone contacted me with a request, but I didn't pursue publicity or market the bears in any way.

I started to see how making bears without pressure could be an entirely different experience from mass production. I often contemplated the bears' purpose, and sometimes prayed for their recipients, particularly for those grieving or in great pain—women going through divorce or getting out of prison, those who suffered from addiction or molestation, families who lost their homes to fire, children who had lost a parent. However, my heart continued to ache most deeply for the women who'd lost their children. I desperately wanted to reach out to them, and sometimes I could, but only in small ways. My own pain continued to get in the way.

One would think, considering 20 years had passed since I lost Tiffany and Matthew, (and because I haven't mentioned them in a few chapters), that the pain of losing them had ebbed somewhat. However, it hadn't. I still couldn't think of them without tears welling up, and if I talked about them at all, I'd come unglued. Every time I heard another bereaved mother talk about her pain, somewhere in my heart I knew telling my story could help her, but I just couldn't seem to talk about my children. It puzzled and saddened me.

Then one Sunday, after listening to Pastor Bryan's sermon about fasting and praying for the answers we sought, I wondered perhaps if fasting could help me identify this wall I kept running up against.

So I fasted, and during my prayer time I poured my heart out to God, as if he didn't already know all about me. On the third day I found myself slipping into familiar territory, mourning over my lost babies. I fell to the floor, sobbing.

God, it's been so long! But it may as well have been yesterday, for all this pain. I just can't get over them. I keep falling apart! What's wrong with me?

And I heard him, very quietly, as if caressing me with his voice.

"Cathy, you have never forgiven me."

I—what?

I couldn't have been more shocked if he had slapped me across the face. The realization made me bolt upright.

I'm still angry. At God. Oh my goodness, I didn't even realize!

Sure, my wounds had been gradually healing, but, in not forgiving God, I had essentially been ripping off the scab every time I remembered the babies, making the pain raw again. Total healing was impossible under these conditions. Overwhelmed by revelation, I fell back down, face to the floor, and sobbed.

Oh God, I'm so sorry. Of course I forgive you. I know you have a good plan for me and the babies just aren't part of it. I don't understand, but I hold no anger or bitterness toward you, God.

As I sobbed, a new prayer began to form.

And please forgive me, God, for keeping this in so many years. Please take this hurt from me. I hold no claim to it anymore.

Twenty years of pain started flowing out of my heart like melting rock, as if the bricks I'd taken such care to stack and re-stack over the years were sinking into a pool and draining away. In many ways, that moment gave me the first awareness that I'd even been nurturing such a wall, because its absence left a lightness I couldn't ignore. On that day, my true healing began.

In the days that followed, although I still think of my babies with sadness, and occasionally shed a tear or two for the lives that never were, I don't experience the heart-numbing pain I'd felt for 20 years. I can smile and talk about them now, without falling apart.

Ryan invited me *and* his birth mom to his wedding in 2012. Although I'd raised him since he was 5, I worried he might feel uncomfortable having us both there. However, he thought nothing of it. He sat me in the front row at the ceremony, ordered a corsage for me to wear, and included me in all the family photos.

At the reception, his mom and I were seated back-to-back at separate tables. After the meal, the emcee's voice blared over the scene, announcing the father daughter dance, but with a twist.

"All right everyone, we are going to do something different tonight. The groom will now dance with his mom while the bride dances with her father."

Strains of "My Wish for You," by Rascal Flatts began to waft through the air, a song that echoed prayers I'd shared with him his entire childhood. Ryan, so handsome in his Marine Corps dress blues, started walking toward the two of us. His mother and I turned in our seats, and our shoulders almost touched as we watched him approach. It was a most awkward moment.

Is he looking at me or his mom?

Trying to contain my nerves took all I had.

Oh Ryan, who was there all those years? Who loves you more than the moon?

As Ryan neared, he grinned his most impish grin and turned to me, reaching for my hand. I've never felt so much pride than in that moment when he pulled me to my feet.

"Oh, Ryan, my heart's going to burst."

He leaned in and whispered, "I thought you'd like this song." We danced the entire song, I with tears flowing freely, while he grinned. That moment will always be one of my favorite memories.

Throughout 2012, God began opening doors again for the bear ministry, sending me orders, one or two at a time, and teaching me to trust again. Once or twice I spoke about my experience, and how I'd found healing. I made a bear every three months or so, primarily memory bears—scraps of clothing belonging to a person who'd passed, so their loved ones had a bear made of familiar material.

Near the end of summer, Sierra's youth group decided they wanted to do something for the children in the pediatric unit at the nearby Cabell Huntington Hospital, where the church youth pastor worked as a physical therapist. He thought the young patients would enjoy a visit and asked if I'd help organize the event.

I jumped at the opportunity, mainly because I wanted Sierra to experience the thrill of giving back to the community. When the pastor said he estimated we would greet about 30 patients, I suggested we bring bears.

In the storage unit I found at least 40 bear patterns we'd cut before the big crash.

From the Remnants

Very funny, God. Do I need to ask what you're trying to tell me?

We put more than 30 bears together over the next few weeks, and gave one to each child. They accepted their new friends eagerly, many holding them tightly and rewarding us with broad smiles. I could see on Sierra's face that she felt the bug—that warm flood of joy that comes in the midst of bringing God's love to others.

"These bears are absolutely wonderful." A parent of one of the patients who received a bear picked up her daughter's blue and green patchwork bear and gave him a squeeze. "What are they made of?"

"Nothing but recycled material." I smiled. "All donated."

She looked thoughtful for a moment and then said, "You know, a man who lives near me has been talking about giving away some material. His grandmother recently passed, and he's clearing away her belongings. Bags and bags of stuff. I think he said he was going to throw it in the trash."

Oh, no. Not again, Lord. I'm not in the business anymore. Don't make me go get it.

But God stayed silent. I fought him as best I could, but it was no use, of course. I just couldn't stop picturing all that material getting thrown away. I knew that was God's way with me . . . bringing up the same thoughts repeatedly.

So there I was the next day, backing up my car to the garage outside his place. His grandmother's craft room had been located above the garage and was filled with bright material, rolls of ribbon, and colorful buttons. I loaded totes and totes of craft supplies into my car, until, once again, my world spilled over with an abundance of cloth and buttons.

In the back of my mind I was also acknowledging the greater message. God used this moment to reassure me that if I stepped out again, he would again provide whatever I needed. He kept at me in little ways. I'd be walking through a thrift store and see a dress or material and think, "Oh, my, that would make a nice bear."

Truth be told, I received only encouragement any time I tried to explain my reluctance to make bears.

To offset extra expenses during this time, I took on a part time job at the YMCA. I met a young writer there named Daniel Foster who would come to the Y to work out on the treadmill. We talked in the evenings while I was working. I would say things like, "I used to make teddy bears" or "I used to paint."

One evening, Daniel said, "Cathy, art is not what you do it is who you are. If you used to paint, then paint. If you used to make teddy bears, then make teddy bears. It is who you are."

His words sparked something in me, and I went home that night inspired to create something. I started drawing and painting small pictures, bringing my art to work to show Daniel.

"Very nice. Keep going," he'd say. He's written three books now, and we encourage each other often to keep being who we are.

ABROAD

"But Cathy, you really should go."

"I don't know, Bo. I don't think I'm the mission type."

I stared at my husband's glowing face across the dinner table. He hadn't been able to stop talking about Pastor Bryan's proposal all day. Apparently, our pastor had been conspiring with Pastor Jason, a minister from a neighboring church, about partnering for their Honduras mission project. Pastor Bryan thought it might be a good endeavor for our church to support. He asked if Bo and I would fly to Honduras with Pastor Jason in October to assess the operation. We'd be a regular Caleb and Joshua, checking out the giants.

Honduras? Who the heck goes to Honduras?

My first impression of serving the poor in a foreign land was negative, I'll admit. Envisioning a life amid poor plumbing, bad water, and insects of every variety, I looked up the destination city on the internet, hoping to find a beautiful description. Instead I came across its listing as one of the most dangerous cities in the world—not exactly a selling point.

Thanks, but I'll pass.

From the Remnants

"Tell you what, Bo." I poked a fork around in my chicken casserole. "You go, and I'll stay home. Perhaps I can make and sell enough bears to cover your airfare."

Bo would not be swayed.

"Cathy, you don't know what you're missing. Everyone should go on at least one mission trip." He leaned forward in his chair, his eyes still gleaming. "Tell you what. Go this one time. If you decide you never want to go again, I'll respect that. It's your choice. But first you have to see what you're saying no to."

I've never been able to resist that boyish smile of his.

Many times in the weeks leading up to that trip, I nearly changed my mind, particularly during the mission team pastors' briefing as I listened to their horror stories about what could go wrong for those who aren't careful.

"You can shower in the water, but keep your mouth shut." The pastor read from a long list. "We'll give you a heavy-duty spray for your clothing. Use it daily. Soak your clothes in bug repellent. Only eat what we give you. We know what food is safe to eat, and we'll arrange all meals. Don't eat food offered to you—take it and say thank you, but discretely put it aside, or act as if you're too busy to eat it right then. Don't be fooled by them rinsing the food in water. I repeat, don't drink their water."

Oh Lord, what have we gotten ourselves into?

The moment I stepped off the plane, I wanted to change my mind for another reason. The humidity hit me like a wet towel, and I could barely breathe. My shirt clung to my back within minutes.

West Virginia never gets this kind of hot.

A pastor named Carlos met us at the airport. We'd be staying at a hotel, but wouldn't check in until later in the afternoon. Pastor Carlos had a broad, laughing face that emanated love. He shook my hand warmly, leaving me feeling as if I'd known him for years.

Pastor Carlos took us to the first of many places we'd visit on our mission trip, a small home in town. As soon as we entered, a full realization of our mission hit me as hard as the humidity had earlier. From the cardboard walls and dirt floor to the lack of air conditioning and running water, the house epitomized the poverty we were about to experience. In essence, it was a shell of a house with a patio out front that served as the community church.

Viewing these conditions might have drained me, if not for Pastor Jason's infectious enthusiasm. As he discussed our itinerary and talked about the work we'd be doing, I couldn't help but get excited. When we settled into our hotel room that evening (a seriously substandard establishment by U.S. standards), I had to laugh at God's sense of humor.

"You know, Bo." I scanned a table top for life forms before setting down my bag. "I always said one day I'm going to travel the world, but my idea of travel was five-star resorts and spas, not this."

Bo's grin hadn't waned all day. "Only the best for you, my queen."

We lost the second day of mission work to illness. Members of our team dropped like flies, and even Pastor Jason and our interpreter, Pastor Jose, found themselves stuck in their hotel rooms hooked up with intravenous fluids provided by our medical team. Bo and I were fortunate not to catch whatever ran through the team, and the sickness passed quickly. By day three, I was eager to get out of that hotel room and ready to work.

Our first task was to visit an outpost where we'd hand out the supplies we'd brought with us. Though some members of our 30-person team were medical and counselling personnel, most were like Bo and me, ready to pitch in wherever we were needed. Early in the morning, we boarded a rickety bus to the mission site.

News of our arrival had passed, primarily through word-of-mouth, to towns across the region, but we had no idea how many people would have received the message. As we rode, I tried to imagine what life must be like in such a desolate area. We'd been driving for hours along a dirt road in what seemed like the middle of nowhere when we passed a young woman balancing a baby on her hips as she walked alongside an older woman. I wondered where they could have come from, or where they could possibly be heading, as I saw no buildings in any direction and we'd not passed any towns in quite some time.

Eventually we pulled up at what looked like the shell of a church with a small pavilion for shade. The line of people already waiting staggered my imagination.

Where did they all come from?

We quickly set up stations and established a numeric system for our visitors. As people came through the doors, each took a number and then went to the first station, where members of our prayer team prayed over them. Then, as their numbers were called, they'd report to the medical and dental area for a checkup and receive whatever treatment the doctors were equipped to handle. Then they'd come to my area, where we'd pass out clothing, food (bags containing flour, rice, beans and lard—enough to feed a family of four for a week), and basic hygiene supplies while they waited to pick up their prescriptions from the makeshift pharmacy.

At one point, as I handed a bag of toiletries to a teenaged boy, I turned to watch two weary travelers approach the back of the number line. Something about them seemed familiar. Astonished, I realized these were the women we'd passed on the road on our way here! They must have walked an hour since we passed them, and many hours before that. I later learned they were mother and daughter. They made it to the front of the line at about 10 a.m. and took a number.

My heart surged with compassion for everyone I met that day. I fell in love with these precious people from the moment the first of them stepped up to my station. Their children were so well behaved; I wanted to cry for what they endured. Most of them sat in line for hours in the heat and humidity without fussing or crying. I never saw any of them give their parents trouble.

In fact, the people were so nice that I quickly learned not to use the few Spanish words in my vocabulary. If I said anything at all, they'd think I knew the language and start talking a mile a minute, leaving me shaking my head helplessly. Instead, I used the universal language of smiles and hugs.

They'd flash those broad white grins and shyly use the one phrase we had in common: "Thank you." The profound gratitude they expressed for the smallest toy (or even a toothbrush, for Pete's sake), left me speechless. Their faces—their eyes, mostly—reflected a sweet tenderness and internal gentleness like nothing I'd ever experienced.

Dear God, I've never seen people with so little be so grateful for almost nothing. Thank you for bringing me here.

As the day wore on, more than 800 people passed through my line, leaving me with next to nothing in my give-away pile. Yet, the line still stretched. The mission team had to turn away hundreds of people who had trekked through the countryside for assistance. The lead pastor said later that we couldn't have seen them all even if we'd stayed two more days, there was so much need.

My heart broke as I watch two small, shoeless girls approach my station with smiles on their dirty faces, hair snarled beyond anything that could be fixed with a comb, and wearing dresses that were way too small. They spoke to the interpreter, who said, "All they want are some flip-flops. Do you have any at all?"

I fought back my tears. They needed everything, but asked only for shoes, and I couldn't help them. I pulled out the last item I had: a huge dress, big enough to fit their mother, who stood behind them. I pantomimed that perhaps she could sew it into two smaller dresses. They smiled sweetly and said "Thank you," and skipped away with their prize.

Crestfallen and greatly shaken, I pulled Pastor Jason aside. "This is horrible, pastor. I don't know what we have to do to make it happen, but we have to get more supplies out to these people. I can't look in babies' eyes and say no, ever again."

I adopted those two girls in my heart. That night and just about every day after I returned from that trip I prayed, *Please Lord, take care of my girls. They desperately need help. Send someone to find them. I know I won't see them again, but you know where they are. Please help them.*

We started packing equipment and loading it onto the bus. In the setting sun I saw the woman with the baby and her mother start back up the road. The pastor said the mother had been able to see the doctor, but that was all. They received their medicine and food bag but had not eaten all day, and wouldn't be able to use the food we'd given them as it required cooking.

"Oh, that's so sad." I watched the dust rising in small clouds around their feet and hoped they'd at least eaten something. "I can't believe they now have to walk all that way back in the dark."

"Yes, it's sad," said the pastor. "Regrettably, the ones we turn away are usually the ones who travelled the furthest to get to us and were last to get in line. A lot of times, they're the ones who are most needy."

From the Remnants

The bittersweet memories of that day changed my life forever. I can no longer view poverty from an outsider's perspective. Before, when I saw poverty on television, I could switch the channel, but now that I've looked in their eyes, and into their "homes," I can't turn it off. Nor do I want to. More on that later.

Throughout the week that followed, as we visited other towns and institutions, I experienced some of the highest and lowest points imaginable on an emotional scale.

At one stop, we visited a Honduran prison unlike anything I've ever heard of in the United States. Essentially, the prison is a walled portion of the city, sealed off by the government. After leaving our identification cards at the gate, we passed through two doors: one maintained by the government and a second, internal door, maintained by the prisoners. The scene inside resembled an impoverished inner-city bazar, with businesses and alleyways in every direction. Men and women were buying and selling from each other, and visiting family members mingled freely with the inmates.

I learned that the government leaves these inmates to fend for themselves. They make and sell products to earn spending money, or family members bring them food. No guards are stationed within the prison. Should a riot break out, the government would simply close the doors and wouldn't allow anyone in until order is restored. That meant no food or supplies because the government doesn't feed them or care for them. The estimated prison population was 2,400 men, 100 women, and countless rodents.

Our mission team entered the prison and set up a church service at a courtyard pavilion in the center of "town." I have to admit, I worried that the guards couldn't stop inmates from hurting us if they wanted to. However, the mission team moved with confidence and authority, as if hanging out with prisoners were the most natural activity in the world. I pushed my fears aside as best I could. As soon as our first notes of praise and worship rang out, a crowd gathered around us and started singing along, dancing in the streets with upraised arms, and making me feel somewhat more at ease despite all the rats running around in the rafters.

After the church service, the team leader banged on the door and we went through an identification process to be let out. I left the prison exhilarated from the experience, and on fire to tell more people about the love of Jesus.

In another town, we held a crusade on an outdoor stage. I stood to the side and watched people fill the streets as far as I could see, dancing to praise and worship music. It gave me a fleeting glimpse of what Heaven could look like, with everyone praising God together.

Those were the highs of our visit. The low point came at the youth detention center. At first, we saw mainly teenagers, between the ages of 13 and 18 or so, whom I presumed were troubled teens caught shoplifting or operating in gangs. But then I saw the babies. Young children, five and six years old. Locked up like criminals!

One of the center officials explained that these were children whose impoverished parents might have left them. They might have been caught stealing food to survive, or running for a gang that recruited them with promises to care for them. Sometimes, desperately impoverished parents even sold them.

As I walked between the cells, a line of small hands extended through the bars. They wanted to be touched. Then we gathered in a meeting room, where sweet little boys as young as my grandson were clinging to my legs, eager for the slightest affection. I thought I would die from sadness!

Despite the lice, which was visible in their hair, I leaned in as close as I could, and I hugged them with all I had. And I prayed.

God, I don't want lice, but you're going to have to protect me because I do not care. What they need is much more important.

By the time we reached the end of the line, Bo had to hold me up.

"They're just babies!" I wailed. "This is just so wrong!"

He practically dragged me onto the bus, where I collapsed in tears. Another event I'll never forget.

Back at the hotel, we had to undergo lice treatment and cover our bodies with a scabies cream for our trip home the next day. I climbed into the bed, white with the sticky cream and wearing a shower cap filled with lice powder.

Bo looked at me with a big, silly grin.

"So, Hon, how do you like this spa treatment?"

"You are SO not funny." I laughed and then fell quiet as I tried to take in everything that had happened in such a short amount of time. Five minutes later I spoke again.

"Next time we have to do more."

"Next time?" He raised an eyebrow.

"Yes." I had never felt more certain. "Bo, we need to come back."

His grin widened. "I know."

※ ※ ※ ※ ※

As I watched Bo from the edge of the pavilion, my heart brimmed with pride and joy. By this point, we'd been back to Honduras many times, and each time I found something new to wonder about. Today it was Bo. Despite the pouring rain, he stood in the center of a large crowd, one hand on a young man's shoulder and the other held upward as he prayed. I didn't need to hear the prayer to understand the scene, as wonder, hope, and light spread from face to face. Tears flowed down the man's gaunt cheekbones and mingled with the rain as he repeated Bo's prayers and gave his life to the Lord.

That's who Bo is! God has answered our prayers! Praise God, this is who he was meant to be!

Even though I'd been praying for years for Bo to realize his calling, I almost missed it. God had taken Bo on a long, painful journey to get there, but neither of us could doubt the destination was well worth the trip.

Needless to say, Bo and I made many return trips to Honduras both together and alone. Bo enjoys praying for and with the people he meets, and has led many to accept Christ as their Lord and Savior. I tend to feel more at home helping people find clothing, food, and other services.

On my second visit to the country, we picked up our work at the same village where we'd run out of supplies a year earlier. I'd prayed for those two sweet girls many times throughout the year, that they'd been able to find shoes and that their mother had found means to provide the care all three of them so desperately needed. It kept me up some nights, the wondering.

So, when I looked up from the donation station and saw my girls laughing and skipping toward me, I could hardly contain my delight. God had answered my prayers to the letter!

The girls were clean and seemingly well-fed, wearing dresses that fit and hair combed into neat ponytails. I pulled out a dress for each of them loaded them up with toothbrushes and soap and everything else in my supply arsenal. Then I asked a friend to take a picture of their beautiful, smiling faces, which later I framed and set alongside my other family photos.

The mission trips have seen great successes. People in that area are not only flourishing, but are coming to Christ in significant numbers. In fact, Pastor Carlos' flock has outgrown his church. On a recent visit, our entire mission team climbed to the top of a mountainous property, where he claimed the surrounding land as far as we could see. We hope to see a larger church there soon, and a community center.

Other on-going projects include building a half-way house for newly released inmates, and improving medical access in the region. Regarding that second endeavor, God couldn't help but show off as he led us in a Gideon sort of way.

The mission team had been planning to build on a foundation that had been previously laid, and turn it into a clinic, but couldn't seem to get the project off the ground. One pastor involved actually backed out of the project, claiming a spirit of confusion had blanketed the place.

It seemed odd, because we honestly felt we were expected to have a clinic there. The construction volunteers returned to the United States, not having built anything that year.

Then a doctor who worked with the mission team "just happened" to drive by an eight-building medical complex that had a for sale sign on it—only a few miles down from where we'd been trying to build. Better yet, the company offering the sale was headquartered across the street from Pastor Jose back in the United States!

As soon as he heard, Pastor Jose walked across the street and started negotiations. Five months later, the company decided not to sell, but to *give away* the 4-million-dollar complex to our mission team. (Bo now serves on the board of directors for the hospital.) They apologized for leaving broken x-ray machines behind, but said perhaps we could sell them. Were we surprised when some technicians on one of our teams cleaned the machines and they worked perfectly? No, we were not, because God is just that good.

Last year I brought a bear with me to give to Anita, a little girl who I learned was sick in the hospital. Her sweet, infectious smile tugged at my heart. As always happens when I witness the love of Christ being passed to someone through a bear that I made, a familiar thought crossed my mind:

. . . And this is who I'm supposed to be.

REMNANTS

After every mission trip I return to the land of plenty, where tooth brushes and flip-flops are taken for granted, and I find myself in awe of the incredible blessings we have in this country. Even people considered impoverished in the United States have far more than they know. They can turn to food pantries and shelters, Federal and civic programs, food stamps, and myriad other resources for help, but in other countries there is so little help available, and so little hope.

This revelation has made me feel a bit like an outsider sometimes, knowing that people I meet every day are going about their lives oblivious to the needs around them. I hold no condemnation. I, too, had been oblivious before that first trip.

God has used even this experience to renew that sense of purpose and compassion for others that has been part of me since childhood. It is with no small sense of surprise that I realize I'm hooked on serving others, and I like it.

I've also had my eyes opened to the incredible amount of waste we take for granted in our society. While I've always had a heart for recycling, my efforts have barely scratched the surface of what's possible. We throw away tons of materials every day that, in a pair of creative hands, can be re-purposed in useful and sometimes lifesaving ways for people in need.

The Honduras missions have served as some of the last pieces of a complex puzzle in which I'm beginning to see the Designer's picture come through. Today, when I look back on all the dreams, the visions, the lean years, the odd jobs, the bear ministry, the disappointments, and even, to a small extent, how Tiffany and Matthew had changed the trajectory of my life (and I wonder if perhaps this *was* God's purpose for them, because without them, the bear ministry would not exist), I can now see all of these events as part of God's plan to prepare me for his purpose.

The same goes for Bo, who became an ordained pastor in June 2015. The trials he endured on his journey strengthened his faith and gave him the tools he needs to help others today. He and I attended ministry training together, but I waited for a year, thinking it wasn't time yet. I started as a licensed minister in 2015 and became an ordained pastor in June 2016 through In the Light Ministries at their East Coast conference.

Sierra graduated high school in 2015, and enrolled in Morehead State University in Kentucky to pursue a degree in animal science in keeping with her passion for working with horses.

Ryan and his wife Kal-le plan to produce a series of children's books based on "The adventures of Tiffy and Matty Bear," which highlight escapades of our grandsons Nash and Anson to teach lessons about kindness.

In April 2016, I led Brian in a prayer to give his life to the Lord. Brian is now on a journey to discover God's plan for his life, and I pray he finds the peace he so earnestly longs for. Chris is still watching from the sidelines, but I pray for him always.

I have resumed my bear-making ministry and I have reestablished the business. I've also created a website, **www.fromtheremnants.com**, for selling the bears online. I hired the mother of that sweet Honduran girl, Anita, who spends much of her time in the hospital. The money she makes sewing bear patterns will help pay for Anita's medical care and help us expand our ministry.

But there's more. So much more.

Cathy Schrader

I believe the image I saw during a meeting years ago that I scribbled into my note pad depicts something with potentially grand significance.

Picture with me, a magnificent warehouse and recycling center, where truckloads of no-longer useful products arrive every day. Those items are sorted for ministry purposes, dismantled and divided by function and substance into bins: doll eyes and puppy noses, wires, plastic, wood, wheels, springs, cloth, ribbons, tubes, clips, and glass . . . Nothing goes to waste.

Then imagine the creative discussions we could have over these supplies. Imagine a room for training people how to restore furniture or make backpacks from canvass and mesh. Or teddy bears from cloth and bunting.

As we continue to imagine, we see these projects leave the center from its distribution bay, being loaded back onto trucks and carried away to be sold at a low cost to those who can afford it, and given away to those who can't. What money does come in goes immediately back into sustaining the operation.

The potentials here are mind-numbingly infinite: The low overhead from working with donated materials, the environmental benefits, the jobs created, and the blessings we could bring to people both in impoverished nations and in our own back yards who can receive God's loving touch through a gift that meets each person's basic need.

I pray God will let me see this place come to fruition. I also pray that Chris will one day see how powerfully God worked in my life, and in Brian's, and that he will find the courage to take the same leap of faith and relinquish control of his life to receive what the Lord has planned for him.

That is the purpose of this book, not just for Chris but for anyone who is wrestling with their faith because of a painful past. I want this book to show how, in one seemingly hopeless, helpless defining moment, God can set someone on a trajectory to live a life bigger and more amazing than anything we could possibly ask or imagine, and how he pieces together what we might see as the remnants of our trials to create a seamless work of beauty we can share with others as evidence of his love and goodness.

From the Remnants

Bo and I have only gratitude for the time we spent in the fiery furnace, and for the joy we feel today. Our lives are fuller and richer after the experience than they ever could have been otherwise.

Because he tested us, and we came forth as gold.

Has this story stirred your heart to learn more about Jesus?

God loves you and wants you to know him. You may not always understand his plan for your life, but you can be sure that he works your life experiences together for your good, and he has prepared a beautiful future for you.

However, you cannot know him without Jesus. We all become separated from God because man's nature is sinful, and God cannot be where sin is present. Jesus Christ bridged that gap by taking the punishment for our sins (death) on his shoulders so that we may be forgiven and live forever with God.

The Bible tells us that, "If you confess with your mouth that Jesus is Lord and believe in your heart that God raised him from the dead, you will be saved." We each must individually ask for forgiveness and receive Jesus as our Savior and Lord. Taking this step doesn't guarantee a trouble-free life, but it does mean that you will never walk alone.

The prayer below can help you start your journey. Once you've prayed this prayer, find a Bible-believing church in your neighborhood and ask for further help. There is much more to discover than we can put in these pages.

Lord Jesus, I do believe You are the Son of God, that You died on the cross to pay the penalty for my sin, and that God raised you from the dead. Please forgive my sins, and make me a part of the family of God. Help me forgive others who have come against me. Come into my life, and take control of it.
Thank you for Your gift of eternal life and for Your Holy Spirit, who has come to live in me. Help me to hear your voice as I submit my life to you for you to lead and to guide me.
I ask this in Jesus' name, Amen.

If you said this prayer today, please consider letting Cathy know by sending her a note on her web page: www.fromtheremnants.com

Bible Verses Referenced in this Book

Scripture quotations marked (NIV) are taken from the Holy Bible, New International Version®, NIV®. Copyright © 1973, 1978, 1984, 2011 by Biblica, Inc.™ Used by permission of Zondervan. All rights reserved worldwide. www.zondervan.com The "NIV" and "New International Version" are trademarks registered in the United States Patent and Trademark Office by Biblica, Inc.™

Scripture quotations marked (NKJV) are taken from the New King James Version. Copyright © 1982 by Thomas Nelson, Inc. Used by permission. All rights reserved.

Isaiah 61:1-3 -- *The Spirit of the Sovereign LORD is on me, because the LORD has anointed me to proclaim good news to the poor. He has sent me to bind up the brokenhearted, to proclaim freedom for the captives and release from darkness for the prisoners, to proclaim the year of the LORD's favor and the day of vengeance of our God, to comfort all who mourn, and provide for those who grieve in Zion—to bestow on them a crown of beauty instead of ashes, the oil of joy instead of mourning, and a garment of praise instead of a spirit of despair. They will be called oaks of righteousness, a planting of the LORD for the display of his splendor.* (NIV)

Jeremiah 29:11 -- *For I know the plans I have for you, declares the Lord, plans to prosper you and not to harm you, plans to give you hope and a future.* (NIV)

Job 23:10 -- *But He knows the way that I take; When He has tested me, I shall come forth as gold.* (NKJV)

Joel 2:25-26 -- *I will repay you for the years the locusts have eaten. . . You will have plenty to eat, until you are full, and you will praise the name of the Lord your God, who has worked wonders for you...* (NIV)

Matthew: 6:25-34 -- *"Therefore I tell you, do not worry about your life, what you will eat or drink; or about your body, what you will wear. Is not life more than food, and the body more than clothes? Look at the birds of the air; they do not sow or reap or store away in barns, and yet your heavenly Father feeds them. Are you not much more valuable than they? Can any one of you by worrying add a single hour to your life?*
"And why do you worry about clothes? See how the flowers of the field grow. They do not labor or spin. Yet I tell you that not even Solomon in all his splendor was dressed like one of these. If that is how God clothes the grass of the field, which is here today and tomorrow is thrown into the fire, will he not much more clothe you—you of little faith? So do not worry, saying, 'What shall we eat?' or 'What

shall we drink?' or 'What shall we wear?' For the pagans run after all these things, and your heavenly Father knows that you need them. But seek first his kingdom and his righteousness, and all these things will be given to you as well. Therefore, do not worry about tomorrow, for tomorrow will worry about itself. Each day has enough trouble of its own." (NIV)

Philippians 1:6 – *...being confident of this, that he who began a good work in you will carry it on to completion until the day of Christ Jesus. (NIV)*

Philippians 4:13 -- *I can do all things through Christ who strengthens me.* (NKJV)

About the Author

Cathy (Berkenkemper) Schrader is a native of West Virginia. She is a wife, mother of three, and grandmother of four. As an ordained pastor of In the Light Ministries, she has served as a missionary in Honduras since 2012. Working as a professional community and economic developer in West Virginia for 20 years, Cathy has been involved in many community restoration projects and programs to help families in need. She loves art, spending time with her family, and serving God to help others.

As a motivational Speaker, Cathy delivers a message of hope with her story of how, at a time of profound loss, God turned her defining moment into a defined destiny. She encourages others to never give up, inspiring her audiences with the story of how God used a teddy bear to change her life, along with the lives of many others. Contact Cathy for speaking engagements at **www.fromtheremnants.com**.

Cathy's Comfort in Christ bears can be purchased at the above web site as well.

From the Remnants

About the Writer

Rosemarie Fitzsimmons is a Rhode Island native who left home at 17 to join the Marine Corps for "just a few years," because, despite dreams of becoming a writer like Laura Ingalls Wilder, she had no means to pay for college. It turned into a 20-year career, primarily as a Combat Correspondent (journalist). Her first book, "Caged Sparrow" won a 2016 Selah award (recognition for Christian writers). As The Portrait Writer, she now writes about God's touch in the lives of every-day heroes, Rosemarie lives with her husband, Jerry, in northern Virginia. They have two sons, Jerry and Charles, and a slightly unstable Egyptian Mau named Aslan.

Made in the USA
Middletown, DE
19 September 2016